D1282440

LARA MACGREGOR

A HOPEFUL LIFE

LEARNING TO HOLD FEAR AND JOY IN THE SAME HAND AT THE SAME TIME

Lara MacGregor

PUBLISHED BY HOPE SCARVES

Kindle Direct Publishing

WWW.HOPESCARVES.ORG

Published by Hope Scarves with Kindle Direct Publishing

First edition 2022

Edited by Laura Ross • Design by Hannah Schiller

ISBN #979-8-218-11079-6

10 9 8 7 6 5 4 3 2 1

DEDICATION

To Team Mac, always and forever

PROLOGUE

A NOTE FROM LARA

I have always tried to capture moments. When I was in 5th grade I started filling in the squares of a cat calendar with the events of the day; a sleepover at Laura's, or a funny thing Gary said in science. For years I recorded the happenings of all 365 days of my life. I also kept diaries, boxes of them. Then, I got my first camera and started capturing moments in film. Inspired by the movie, *Reality Bites* in 1994, I hauled around a giant shoulder held video camera to capture the moments of our senior year.

This book is my newest way to capture who I am. I don't want to be forgotten.

I was born in the small town of Whitehall, Michigan in 1976. My childhood was closely connected to the water, sailing, swimming, dune climbing, sunsets. The first 25 years of my life I lived within five miles of Lake Michigan.

I grew up in a safe, loving home with my parents, Art and Sue Plewka, and my little brother Eric. My dad literally built our home around us as we grew up. We lived in a timber frame, with the frame of the house built in the tradition of a barn raising in a weekend workshop, engaging craftsmen and artists from across the country. Instead of nails, the frame is held together with large wooden pegs. Then, my dad finished the house for the rest of my childhood - framing, and more. Today, I marvel at the perseverance and patience my mom and dad applied to this unconventional building experience and my consequential childhood.

My parents were both teachers, so every summer we went on extended road trips to national parks and far off places. Before technology stole our gaze, we marveled out the window, eagerly completing the workbooks and road trip games my mom assembled for our adventures. We made our way through the mountains and to the coasts, camping along the way. When I became a teenager I was often disappointed to have to leave my friends. "But, everyone but me is going to be at Chris' pool party!" Rolling my now 45-year-old eyes, I know these adventures planted a love of traveling in me from a young age. It wasn't until I was at Hope College (And yes, I see the irony in Hope College, it's a great liberal arts school in Holland, Michigan) deciding on my major, that I realized some grown ups didn't get summer vacation. I immediately signed up for education classes. But, my passions ultimately led me in a different direction and I had to accept the adult reality of two weeks' vacation.

Luckily, I met a cute boy who loved to pack adventure and new experiences into weekends just as much as I did. My husband Jay and I met shortly after college through a mutual friend. At first we were just running buddies, until he finally convinced me to go on a date that didn't involve exercise. A year later, we were camping on the shore of Lake Michigan on Beaver Island. He asked me to go for a walk and in the sand were the words "Will you marry me?" He gave me the most beautiful ring and we dove in the freezing cold waves to avoid the black flies swarming our celebration.

We were married in 2000. It poured on our July wedding day. I got in a hydroplaning car accident with my bridesmaids on the way to the salon. Our plans for a beautiful boat ride from the church to the reception were ruined. Our outdoor reception was almost swamped by heavy rain. As if foreshadowing our life together, we made the best of it. And, after so much went wrong, the sun eventually came out. It was beautifully muddy, the crisp after-the-storm air making way for a gorgeous sunset.

Jay and I pictured raising a family in West Michigan. We built a home a short walk from Lake Michigan. We spent our days building our careers, me working toward a Masters in Public Administration with a focus on nonprofit leadership while I was working at the United Way. Jay got his MBA while building his career in business and manufacturing. Our nights and weekends were packed with training for triathlons, fishing, sailing, and camping.

But, life took us far beyond familiar. We lived overseas a bit in Liverpool, England, then Birmingham, Alabama before moving to Louisville, Kentucky. We began a family. Each stop added experiences, perspectives and friends to our life. I'm grateful for each twist and turn of our story.

When I was about 10 years old, my friend Heather and I were playing in the woods around my house. We laid in the ferns dreaming about what we wanted to be when we grew up. Like most little girls with big plans I said, I want to be famous.

"How will you know you are famous?" Heather asked.

I responded, "A lot of people will care when I die."

That's kind of a bizarre perspective for a 10-year-old.

I have no idea why I said it. But, I remember the conversation clearly and think about that a lot these days. So many people care about me. I guess you could say my childhood dreams are coming true.

I've spent my life capturing moments so I didn't forget them. I hope this book helps you to never forget me.

My Hopeful Life is
a collection of my personal essays. I
have been writing my whole life, in journals, in
the early days of email, tucking slips of paper into a
shoe box, in college creative writing courses, on a blog
I created when cancer entered the picture, and now finally,
in a real book!

Our stories connect us. They bridge generations and help us understand things outside our own circle. They bring perspective to our lives. They also capture who we are to preserve forever. In an age of 20 second sound bites, vanish mode, and 24-hour news cycles, permanence brings me peace.

Crafting this book is a gift to many. This first section is for everyone, in particular, our sons, Wills and Bennett, and their dad, Jay. I know their lives will move on in beautiful and brutal ways when I am no longer here physically, but I hope my story will help them know me more as they grow up.

When I was writing these essays I tried to answer one singular question. I asked, "How can I live a Hopeful Life, regardless of what comes next?"

I hope as you read my stories you feel the answer to this question both for myself, for you, and for all of us.

WHEN THE WORLD COMES CRASHING DOWN

"You have cancer."

I was 30 years old, and seven months pregnant when I first heard the words, "You have cancer."

Life was pretty amazing for our young family. Jay and I were renovating a historic home, chasing after our vivacious, blonde two-year-old, Wills, and growing our professional careers. We were active triathletes, with busy social lives and big dreams. And, we were growing our family.

As our second pregnancy progressed, I had some discomfort in my left breast and felt a lump in the shower. Assuming it was a crazy pregnancy change, I added it to my list to discuss at my check up with my OB/GYN.

Later that week, I went for a run and prepared to go to my 7-month pregnancy checkup. Reviewing my list in the waiting room, I was most interested in talking about my hope to have a natural VBAC, or vaginal birth after cesarean. I could already hear Dr. Sharp's joke about "natural childbirth in Alabama means no make-up." I had also found a doula I was hoping to assist us with childbirth this time around. Oh, and there was that little bump. I needed to ask about that. It was probably a milk duct.

After all my other questions were answered, and almost as an afterthought, I asked the doctor about the lump in my left breast and pointed out the blood on the inside of my bra. He stopped in his tracks, laid me down on the crinkly white exam table paper and did a breast exam. He left the room abruptly, returning with instructions to go directly to the 4th floor, where a breast surgeon could see me immediately.

I looked at him incredulously and said, "I'm sorry, what?"

Wills was at childcare for three hours and I had to get to Target and run a couple errands. This was supposed to be a routine checkup for the baby.

What was happening? Why a breast surgeon? I went upstairs in a fog. I snuck out of the busy waiting room and sat on the floor at the end of the hallway, the only quiet place I could find to call Jay at work.

His assurance comforted me immediately. They were probably just taking extra precautions he said, adding, I'm sure it's nothing to worry about. Jay lives life with a strategy he calls PMA, Positive Mental Attitude. I was glad to let it wash over me and ease my fears.

The next thing I knew, my pregnant belly and breast were exposed in an exam chair while a surgeon took a core needle biopsy sample. Explaining it was the only way to know for certain, I left with a very sore boob and in a haze of confusion. "Certain" for what?

I picked up Wills from childcare and went for a walk to the park. I repeatedly reassured myself this must be an overreaction. I was a completely healthy 30-year-old with no family history of cancer.

I chased Wills up and down the slide and held his pudgy little legs as he tried to cross the monkey bars. I was strong, healthy, and expecting a baby. There was so much good in our lives. Soon the bizarre idea of breast cancer moved out of my mind. Surely there was nothing to worry about.

A couple of days later, I was sitting in a salon getting Wills' blonde curls trimmed. He teetered on my knees making room for my pregnant belly. We were both wearing haircut capes and giggling. My phone rang and I answered it to pass time as we waited for our turn.

Confused by the words on the other side of the line, I looked up at the wall of mirrors in front of me. There sat our adorable little boy, patting my pregnant belly. I listened as the doctor said the words "breast cancer." I believe he kept speaking but I don't remember the words.

I felt our world shattering. The confusion was overwhelming. My head was pounding, I couldn't form a response. I was numb with disbelief. Tears were streaming down my face.

I ripped off the salon capes and quickly carried Wills to the bathroom. I sank down the wall of the bathroom, until I found myself on the floor sobbing uncontrollably. Wills put his two little pudgy hands to my cheeks and said, "Mama, do you have a boo-boo?"

I nodded.

I managed to pick myself up from the floor and get us home. I called Jay and he immediately left work, though he had over an hour commute, so it felt like forever until he arrived. Wills and I walked around the park behind our house to keep him happy and occupied while I choked back my sobs.

Jay found us there gathering acorns on a park bench. I fell into his arms and sobbed. At this point, I didn't even really know what I was afraid of. I didn't know anyone close who had faced cancer. To this point in our life, I hadn't been seriously hurt or sick. That was something I had watched other families endure. My life had been pretty lucky.

I was terrified of the unknown. What did this mean? How would this impact our unborn baby? What was to come? Surgeries, chemotherapy, death? I had no idea. I just knew we were no longer living in our happy little world of invincibility. I felt like we were in a free fall. I wasn't sure what to hold on to or how far we were going to fall. I was numb and scared but also naively certain we could "beat it." After all, I ran the Komen 5K, and there were thousands of women there celebrating their survivorship. I didn't know how, but I was certain that was going to be me.

The days that followed were like a bad dream. Doctor appointments filled with words I had never heard before became my reality - estrogen positive, HER2 negative, invasive ductal carcinoma in situ, mastectomy, lumpectomy, words, treatments, decisions. I took notes looking at my hand as if it was detached from my body.

We had second and third opinions and appointments that happened quickly. It moved rapidly, because being young and pregnant was particularly dangerous. On a Saturday morning we strolled Wills to our favorite coffee shop. Sitting outside the café, he sang the Muffin Man song while tearing into his favorite morning glory muffin. Jay and I looked at each other with tired exhaustion.

Just a week ago our biggest decision was the finish on our new kitchen cabinets, and now we were deciding what surgery I would have the coming week. Disbelief hung over us like a shared burden we carried together. We smiled and joked with Wills, along with deep sighs, in between sips of O'Henry's coffee. We went about a typical Saturday for us – a trip to the park, grocery shopping, home projects – all the while on the outside looking like a happy, healthy young family. Yet, everything we thought we knew about our life, our future,and the strength of our bodies seemed broken. It seemed like a mistake; this couldn't be happening to us.

That night a kind man named Dr. Jimmie Harvey called and introduced himself as a friend of a friend who had heard about my story. He offered his assistance as a resource. This kind, gentle voice on the phone answered my lingering questions and offered hope and a path forward that didn't feel sterile or medically overwhelming. It felt like love.

Dr. Harvey would become my oncologist and help us navigate the year to come. Dr. Harvey wore colorful bow ties and round tortoise shell glasses, and he sat and talked with you like you were the only patient on his schedule, a detail the rest of his staff worked hard to manage. His voice was quiet but confident, with a southern accent that sounded like smooth, sweet honey. I had no idea how much trusting an oncologist meant to the experience of cancer care, but, I would come to realize he was the light I needed to help me find my way as I entered the world of cancer.

After much discussion on the best first step, I decided to have a lumpectomy the coming week. A mastectomy felt like way too big of a surgery to do while pregnant, but I wanted to get the mass out. I had been warned that it would be nearly impossible to get clear margins with just a lumpectomy, based on how close the tumor was to the surface and the spider-like tentacles that seeped into the milk ducts. As expected, the lumpectomy wasn't fully successful at removing all the cancer, so days later I started chemotherapy, and was told a complete mastectomy would be necessary following the end of chemo treatment.

Jay and I pulled into the expectant parent parking spot close to the entrance and walked into the oncology unit holding each other's hands tightly. As I signed in at the desk the receptionist looked up with her sweet southern accent and said, "Oh honey, you're in the wrong place, OB/GYN is in the suite down the hall."

My eyes full of tears, I finished signing in my name and looked up at her, "No, ma'am, I'm in the right place."

Moments later, I was having an IV inserted in my right arm as a nurse explained the way they would administer this drug called Adromycin, or "the red devil." It was Kool Aid red, and so toxic they pushed it manually. I listened with my arms gently resting on my very pregnant belly, feeling our unborn child kick.

It was important to me to have a healthy pregnancy. I stopped drinking caffeine, ate lots of leafy greens, avoided alcohol, and drank lots of water. And here I was, pumping toxic chemicals into my body as I felt our baby wriggle inside me. I closed my eyes and tucked my head away from the arm tethered to the red drug. Tears streamed down my cheeks. I bit the inside of my cheek until it bled.

I sat in that chemo chair with our unborn baby for nine rounds of treatment. My hair started falling out after a couple treatments, so on New Year's Eve, we sat on our back porch and two-year-old Wills shaved my head with help from his daddy. He laughed as he blew my hair like a dandelion into the wind. I was glad he was too little to understand what was happening. His life was still so joyful, surrounded by family and friends who loved him through all the treatments and doctor appointments that took us away from him. His laughter reminded us what we were fighting for.

Despite the sadness and fear of the diagnosis, there was so much joy in our house. Dr. Harvey laid out a clear path of treatment and fueled me with his kindhearted hope that I would endure this and come out the other side cancer free. We were all grounded in the hope that we could beat this. Of course, I had hard days, but I was fueled by deep hope and determination that a lifetime of perseverance and problem solving had prepared us for this moment.

NEW LIFE - AND A
NEW WAY OF LIFE

I was strong and the light at the end of the tunnel was brilliant. We had a clear path toward wellness and were on our way to success. Delivering a baby is always a scary, yet exciting, time for parents-to-be but in our case, the stakes were raised. Our son, Bennett, had to be born in between chemo treatments at a point when my counts were high enough to endure delivery. I had a window in which my hopes for a VBAC delivery were still a possibility.

I walked the neighborhood, pregnant and bald, trying to get him to meet my timeline. I ate spicy food, drank Guinness, and did all the things mothers can do to try to get labor moving. Surely, with all I had endured I could have the childbirth I was hoping for, I thought. I had been able to do so many other amazing things with my body, including running marathons and completing triathlons. I loved my strong, capable body. I was in awe of childbirth and always expected my body to be able to experience it.

So much had been taken from us with this cancer diagnosis, leaving us sad and disappointed. I wanted this one "normal" experience at the start of a new life, but, as we watched the window narrow, a C-section was scheduled so we could welcome our babe to this world while also keeping my chemo schedule on track. We previously pivoted on our birth plan with our first born when he was breeched and an emergency C-section was required, so I knew that childbirth was beautiful no matter how it happened.

I faced the disappointment with a good cry in the bathtub, rubbing my very pregnant belly and bald head, which were strangely similar in feeling and firmness. I reassured myself that his birth was part of a much bigger story of me continuing cancer treatment, regaining my health, and raising him. I was so excited to meet him.

Bennett Arthur MacGregor was born full term, healthy, and full of spunk on February 8, 2008. We were worried he would have side effects from chemo, but he was perfect. His scream was music to our ears. I was still strapped to the operating table when Jay brought him around the C-section drape and put his head next to mine. I breathed in the smell of new life. I looked up at Jay, pleading with my eyes, "Is he OK? Is he healthy?"

Jay nodded. Bennett was fine. I breathed a deep sigh of relief for the first time since I heard the word cancer. He was here, outside of my cancer-riddled body. He was safe and whole and well. I don't even remember thinking about cancer. Our lives stood still with bright clarity and love as we experienced the miracle of new life.

When we were finally in our room, I pulled back Bennett's little hat to reveal tufts of red hair. Red hair? In all my dreams of who this little human would be, never did I imagine him with red hair. Neither Jay nor I have red hair in our family. We looked at each other and laughed. Had the "red devil" chemo created a lasting impact from all the treatments and turned his hair red? It was a welcome moment of humor in an otherwise overwhelming and emotional experience of new life. Bennett would grow to fit the "red devil" persona as a feisty, competitive, determined kid. His red hair fits his personality perfectly!

Those first days in the hospital were precious and hard. I was worried about breastfeeding because I loved it so much with our first son, Wills. At the time, it came easily, and we nursed for well over a year. Prior to Bennett's birth, Jay and I discussed how important it would be to make sure no one talked to me about breastfeeding in the hospital. Jay intentionally talked with the nurses daily to make sure everyone knew the circumstances we were facing. There was a sign on the door next to a big blue bow. It was like breastfeeding didn't exist and we moved forward with formula as if that was the only option in the world.

My breasts never produced milk, which was a huge relief. When it was time for Bennett's first feeding, I asked Jay to do it because I worried it would be too hard for me. I watched from my bed as he sat on the uncomfortable hospital couch, carefully holding our little guy in one arm, cradling his head in his hand, gently offering Bennett the tiny one-ounce hospital formula bottle. Bennett's bright eyes locked with Jay's. I wiped away tears as I watched the amazing connection between the two of them, even as my heart ached for the connection that I didn't get to have breastfeeding.

I watched Bennett's eyes close with the satisfaction of nourishment and Jay gently handed him to me. I took a deep breath of Bennett and laid him on my chest. So much was wrong in our little family, but in that moment everything was right.

As our family celebrated this new life, I felt more and more confident that cancer wasn't going to stop us. I looked at this amazing family I was blessed with and determined there was no way I was leaving this world.

I returned to chemo treatment nine days after Bennett was born. My parents were in town from Michigan and watched Wills and Bennett while we were at the appointment. I brought a small album of pictures to share the happy news of Bennett's birth with the nurses and staff. It was passed around the infusion suite for all to see, making the time feel more like a celebration than a treatment as I shared stories of his bright red hair and how great of a baby he was. I was more determined than ever to keep the cancer-fighting machine moving forward so we could move on with life.

Hope was my rock. I knew cancer wasn't going to take all of this away from me. The next chemo drug I had, Taxol, was harder on my body. As we waded through those early weeks of a newborn at home and the emotions of a two-year-old sharing his parents with a baby, my body got sicker and sicker.

We were surrounded by family and friends who helped us through each day. We had an extra helper stay with us for months, a glorious mix of parents, aunts, cousins, friends. An extra set of hands to sanitize baby bottles, keep the laundry on track, snuggle Bennett or play Legos with Wills made all the difference. Meals were delivered every other evening, while friends walked our yellow lab, and neighbors cut our grass.

Bennett and Wills were cared for by many mamas. While I was grateful for the support, It was hard for me to not be the mom I wanted to be. I wanted to be the one to wake up with Bennett in the middle of the night and rock him back to sleep. Yet, as I heard him cry from his bassinet beside my parents' bed in the guest bedroom, I was grateful my fatigued body could roll over and rest.

I loved seeing Wills happy with all the fun that was presented to him during this time, including trips to the circus, new shoes, and face paint at a festival, but I was sad it wasn't Jay and me sharing these outings with him. We were blessed with a revolving door of help and support. It was a delicate balance because we needed the help, and we were grateful for the gift of so much support, but at the same time I wanted to have a moment where it was just the four of us - Team Mac - as we had started calling ourselves. I remembered countless quiet nights just Wills and I rocking and nursing and dreaming of all life had in store for us. I felt robbed of this precious time with our new baby.

Instead of basking in the happy bliss of new motherhood, I was sick and weak from chemo. My nails were falling off. I was bald and pale as the last of my eyebrows and eyelashes fell out. My nose constantly dripped since I didn't have nose hair, but it also burned with extreme dryness. I was rapidly losing weight because I struggled to eat from nausea and everything tasting like metal. Despite all this, I was determined to get my health back. I saw this pain as a temporary chapter in a much bigger story. I would endure whatever was necessary to get my health back and be the mom I wanted to be for a long, long time to come.

While this time in our life was difficult, each day we were moving toward the light at the end of the tunnel, always guided by hope.

When Bennett was three months old, I finally finished chemo and had a double mastectomy. The surgery was more painful than I expected but it was an incredible relief to have taken this big step toward wellness. I came home from the hospital on Mother's Day, welcomed by two beautiful baby boys who needed their mama.

The weeks that followed the surgery came with a lot of tears as I couldn't lift more than five pounds, which meant I couldn't care for my children, again. Wills had to be gentle with mama's "boo-boo" and learned not to jump on me or squeeze me too tightly. His outstretched arms needing to be picked up were answered with me kneeling down next to him and asking if he could walk. He was resilient and accommodating without ever understanding the magnitude of his reality. He quickly learned to run to daddy for piggyback rides, never missing a beat.

In those hard days that followed my surgery and recovery, I remember standing at Bennett's crib, looking down at his flailing arms and legs as his red face grew brighter from his cries. I stood there helplessly unable to reach down over the side of the crib to pick him up and comfort him, the tight bandages still holding my broken body together from surgery. Regardless of the weight restrictions, the limited range of motion in my arms made me unsure if I could safely lift him.

"Mom!" I kept yelling up the stairs, but she had jumped in the shower and didn't hear me or him crying. It only lasted a couple minutes, but I felt the enormity of cancer in that helpless moment. The bandages felt tighter and my legs felt weak as I sunk to the floor and held his little fingers through the bars in his crib reassuring him that I loved him and Nana would be there soon to pick him up.

We had around the clock help from friends and family to ensure my body healed and the boys were loved and cared for. Despite the pain and heartbreak, our home was overflowing with love. No matter what challenge came up each day, we were all grounded on the hope that we were moving forward toward wellness. The future was bright. We had so much to live for.

Slowly my body healed, and I regained my strength. My hair started growing back and stubble of eyebrows and eye lashes started filling back in the face I missed. I walked the boys in the stroller and laid on the ground and played with them. I picked them up and carried Bennett in the baby carrier. I was able to be their mom again!

Later that summer, I had the last surgery to place my permanent implants. I also had my first full body scan to ensure there wasn't cancer anywhere else in my body, which was a test that typically would have been part of the original diagnosis, but was postponed because of our pregnancy.

Dr. Harvey called me himself to tell me there was no evidence of disease in my body. I listened to his slow, steady voice with great anticipation. We had done it. I knew we would. It was a quick call. But in those precious minutes it was like giant glistening doors to our future were opened wide and we could see a bright, healthy future ahead. We were grounded in hope, supported by hundreds, and determined to make it to the other side. We beat cancer.

Jay and I squeezed Wills so tightly he wiggled out of our embrace in laughter. Baby Bennett squawked his pterodactyl shriek in the bouncy seat. I ran to the fridge and grabbed a bottle of champagne and we let the cork fly from our back deck. I couldn't stop my body from jumping, laughing, giggling.

Jay and I stared at each other. The past year had been a whirlwind. We were both stretched to our limits emotionally, physically, and together as a couple. We had screamed and yelled, sobbed, and clung to each other, hoped and feared, together. Yet through it all we both were fiercely determined to find our way through. Deep down, we never doubted, even on the hardest days, that we would make it. We were both just too afraid to say it for fear of things getting worse. That night, as we laughed and celebrated our "victory" we let all that heaviness go. That night we were strong and well and hopeful. We got out the good crystal from our wedding day and toasted all we had endured and the hopes and dreams we had for the future.

As a young family, we had been tested in a way we never imagined. Our eyes and hearts opened to the preciousness and fragility of life. We were determined to raise our boys with a deep sense of gratitude and love. We were excited for the life we had fought for – it was a life of adventure, physical challenges, resilience, and hope.

Let this new life ahead of us begin!

WEATHERING MORE
STORMS AND SEARCHING
FOR THE RAINBOWS

Often, when you are newly diagnosed with breast cancer, you are given a "welcome bag" of sorts. Because I was diagnosed in Alabama (the land of fluffing), my bag was pink with pom-pom trim and a huge embroidered pink ribbon. In it were resources for "beating" breast cancer like lotions, a pink loofah, mini boxing gloves and a water bottle that said, "Save Second Base." I stuffed the bag in the back of my closet. One of the things the bag didn't include was information on PTSD - Post Traumatic Stress Disorder - which would emerge as a resource I needed more than pink boxing gloves.

Following our "alternative reality" year of cancer treatment, I was crowned cancer free and sent back into the world. As I returned to work, friends, and date nights, I realized I was struggling. At first, I hid my pain. I felt I should be grateful. I felt I should be happy. I thought, I am lucky. What was wrong with me?

Eventually, it was too much to hide. I snapped at the kids, I got frustrated easily, and my fuse was short with Jay. I could handle things - until I couldn't. One afternoon, I was trying to get a very lively Bennett down for his afternoon nap. We read three books, sang songs, and rocked in the rocking chair. I laid him in his crib but every time I tried to walk out of the room he started crying. I came back into the room four times, gently laying him on his belly and rubbing his back. He'd lay his head down and close his big blue eyes until I tried to leave the room, then he'd sit up. He needed a nap; I needed a break.

On the fifth time I laid him down forcefully, frustratedly telling him it was time to sleep. He looked up at me confused and big tears rolled down his cheeks. His lip quivered. I sank to the floor in front of his crib sobbing. What was I doing? The anger I felt in that moment scared me. I didn't feel like myself. I knew I needed help. I asked a friend for recommendations on counselors.

A counselor helped me put words to my pain. For the past year I was focused on getting well. I had a road map: surgery, chemo, surgery, chemo, reconstruction. When I walked out of my last treatment, I felt immense relief. But eventually relief turned to grief and anger with feelings I didn't allow myself to feel during treatment. Only now was I processing the enormity of what we had endured.

She explained that what I was feeling was real. I had been to "battle" for my life. I was experiencing post-traumatic stress disorder, PTSD. Just learning there was an explanation for my mood swings helped me relax. I became more aware of my feelings, not ignoring them, but listening to what they meant. I gave myself a break from being the perfect "survivor." There wasn't any one way to live beyond breast cancer. I was able to do this uniquely, in my own way.

Sitting in the counselor's comfortable green velour chair in her bright sunroom full of plants, I processed deep feelings: my fear of dying, the fear of leaving Jay with two young kids, the fear of someone else being their mom, the fear of the cancer coming back. Eventually, I realized cancer had changed me.

Before cancer, I thought my life was unfolding perfectly, a result of my hard work and preparedness. It wasn't without its challenges, but Jay and I both believed our problem-solving skills would get us through any situation. Two years into our marriage we built a house in the dunes of Lake Michigan. We didn't fully know what we were doing, and we made mistakes and we persevered. It was early 2000's and everyone was painting rooms a deep, russet red color. I thought this was the perfect color for our bedroom but when we finished, I looked around and realized it didn't work. The house was on the lake and it needed to be a light blue. Six coats of primer and paint later, several arguments and lots of patience from my husband, we were surrounded by the perfect light grey/blue bedroom. Hints of red peaked out in one of the corners. I liked it there as a reminder of how we made the pivot. These were the kinds of problems I faced throughout my life, solvable problems. I was good at it.

The year facing cancer showed us both that some things are out of our control. Some problems simply can't be solved. This helpless feeling changed our outlook completely. Cancer showed me that I was no longer an invincible woman. My health was fragile. I was vulnerable. Bad things can and do happen.

As I healed, I tried to be the indestructible woman I was before cancer. I wanted to return to my naivete, my blissful belief that with hard work and perseverance you can find your way through any problem. But I wasn't this person. I was vulnerable. I understood life was unpredictable and I didn't want to be broken. I was trying to be strong and whole again.

I remember crying in my backyard one afternoon because I was overwhelmed by these mixed emotions. I laid in the grass, stared up at the blue sky and I started to understand that I wasn't healing, because I was trying to be the person I was before breast cancer. That person didn't exist anymore. I had to become someone new.

Through writing, long runs, counseling sessions, time in nature, and reflecting I began to breathe life into this new woman. I had to let go of the invincible woman I was before. Cancer changed me. I began to heal when I realized I was becoming a different version of myself.

I found joy in welcoming and accepting her. The new me didn't find safety in the perfect, happy ending or the solution to the problem. The new me was vulnerable, scared, and broken, and as a result, I was stronger, braver, deeper, and more authentically living in the messy reality of life. I realized that struggle is part of the story and not something to just get over. It is intertwined in all parts of life.

I also realized how precious the joyful moments in life are - both the simple little moments and the big, special adventures. I cherished it all deeper. I recognized how fragile it all was. Gratitude ran deeper in me than it ever had before cancer.

My hair started growing in, eye lashes sprouted, and my body healed. I went back to work at McWane Science Center. I was excited to get back to my professional obligations of planning the annual gala, Beaker Bash, which raised money for the scholarship program to bring students to the museum. I juggled dropping two little kids off at daycare by 7:30 every morning. It was challenging and I loved it. It no longer felt like a burden, but an opportunity. Jay and I were juggling busy jobs, two little kiddos, grocery runs, and playdates. We were in the whirl of the regular life things we dreamed of. In November 2009, my one year "cancerversary," we packed up our little family in our black Subaru Outback and headed on an adventure in the mountains of North Carolina. We got up bright and early on our first day and hit the trails, Bennett in a hiking backpack, squawking with delight in Jay's ear, and Wills running eagerly ahead on the trail turning sticks into imaginary lightsabers and throwing rocks into the stream. We hiked and laughed and explored. My legs ached with the amazing feeling of exertion.

After a little while we stopped at the base of a waterfall for snacks, an important part of any hike with toddlers. I climbed around on the giant rocks with three-year-old Wills. Then we sat on top of a big rock all together and shared granola bars. I sat in wonder just looking at our little family. There was no one around us, we were deep in the woods of the Nantahala Wilderness. Team Mac, the four of us. We were complete. There was nothing else I wanted in life but to be together with these three guys and see what our future held together. This was what I had fought for, right here, in front of me. I was excited to be their mom, healthy and strong, and ready to embrace what the future held for our family. I knew there would be many more adventures just like this one.

We returned home from our amazing adventure to learn that Jay's dad wasn't doing well.

Throughout my breast cancer treatment, Jay was traveling back and forth to be with his dad, Ken, who was facing cancer in Michigan. He endured 18 months of agonizing treatments and setbacks. Jay balanced being there for him and his family, while also being in Alabama for me and our family.

It was a hard time. Ken died on January 9, 2009. His funeral was February 6th, two days before Bennett's first birthday. I dressed Bennett in a maroon corduroy outfit with a white turtleneck, his wobbly legs still unsteady at walking, as I quietly played with him in the basement of the church. There were so many feelings rushing through my body.

During the service, I held Bennett in my lap, rubbing my short stubble hair as we honored Ken MacGregor's life. I gently held Bennett's little pudgy hands in mine, thinking how this could have been my funeral. Tears dripped on the arms of his crisp white turtleneck.

I thought about the pact Ken and I had made the last time we saw each other. "We'll be on the boat together next summer." We shook on it. He was 66.

Life is fragile.

As if all of this wasn't hard enough, 2009 was also a volatile time in the world economy. Amid caring for me and our family and mourning the loss of his father, Jay faced enormous challenges at work. Days after returning from his dad's funeral, he had the unenviable task of shutting down the business he was president of, which resulted in the layoffs of hundreds of employees. The closing of the company also meant he was without a job.

We sat on our back deck, the one Jay built by hand to save money during the renovation, staring up at the stars. The boys were finally asleep, and we clinked our IPAs in a silent toast. We were grateful Jay was given a relocation opportunity within the larger holding company, when many people were struggling to find employment, but, leaving the community of support, our home, my job, and the safety net we still clung to as we emerged from trauma was daunting.

We were devastated to leave the community that had surrounded us through our tumultuous year of cancer. Our home was a creative outlet and much needed distraction for me during cancer. I loved dreaming about the way this house would tell our story. I saw our family growing up here. The house had so many of our touches, like the boys' rooms side-by-side with a bathroom in between. A creative little secret passage pocket door I worked into the design from our closet to the laundry room. The penny round tile I bravely used as a backsplash in the kitchen though I'd never seen it done before. All these elements were part of our story.

I wrote our names and story on the wooden beams one Saturday afternoon before the drywall went up. The words ALWAYS HOPE in all capital letters became a part of this historic home renovation forever.

WELCOME TO THE 'VILLE

As we faced the enormity of moving to a new city that I wasn't even sure how to pronounce - Loo-a- ville, Loey-ville, Lou-ville, Kentucky, I was given a card that said:

"We are only truly in charge of two things: how we prepare for what might happen and how we respond to what happens. The moment when things actually do happen belong to God."

I couldn't control that I had cancer, that Jay's dad died, or that Jay lost his job and we had to move. However, I could control how I reacted. Jay seemingly modeled this perspective every damn day with his calm, cool, hardworking approach to life. How else could he have endured everything we had faced in the past year? I walked into my beautiful kitchen I worked really hard to design and hated it was going to soon be owned by another family. Jay was washing dishes, I touched him on the shoulder, and as he turned around, I gave him a big hug. "We can do this," I said.

And I started to cry.

Weeks later, our car, towing a U-Haul, pulled out of our sweet home Alabama, stuffed with two kids and a yellow labrador. We drove north. Jay and I both grew up in Michigan, so at least Kentucky was perfectly located six hours closer to home.

We moved into an apartment at first while we looked for a place to call home. A corporate relocation realtor took me and the kids around to different neighborhoods while Jay was at work. She showed me development after development with ponds, swimming pools, and huge closets. I knew this wasn't right. I asked her, "Where is the neighborhood where I can walk to a park and a coffee shop, where there are old established trees, where the houses have small closets, and homes are overpriced?"

She laughed and drove me to Louisville's treasured Fredrick Law Olmsted-designed Cherokee Park. I was instantly in love with the neighborhoods, homes, and vibe. Jay and I laid a folded-out paper map on the hood of our car and decided we would end up somewhere directly connected to the sprawling park system that ran through the center of the city. I found our house after playing in the park with the boys. It needed some work, and the road was a little busier than we hoped, but it sat up on a hill and the location was perfect. That night, Jay and I strolled the boys around the park minutes from our almost house. We counted 22 different sports being played in Seneca Park and we knew we wanted to plop ourselves right in the middle of all of this healthy fun.

While it felt like our family was deeply rooted in our friendships and experiences in Alabama, which was a pivotal time that shaped us, we realized the boys were only one and three years old. The years that followed would see the boys embrace Louisville, Kentucky as their home.

My health continued to hold strong, and I returned to my oncologist for annual checkups perfectly timed with my Alabama friend's beach trip. At my first appointment I brought him a framed picture of Bennett. On the white matte I wrote in a black Sharpie marker, "Dr. Harvey, thank you for my bright red hair." Each year that followed I replaced the 5x7 picture with a new picture of Bennett as he grew up. After several years, I looked forward to the appointment, barely remembering the fear and anxiety that once accompanied the walk to the oncology office. Life was good!

After five years of beach trips and annual checkups, Dr. Harvey told me I didn't have to come back to his office. Stunned, I insisted we still meet at Starbucks when I was in town. I finished the recommended five years of Tamoxifen therapy post-breast cancer treatment. We talked about healthy lifestyle choices, and I was released from his care. I even asked if it was possible to try to have another baby. Was all of this really happening? My cancer treatment was complete, and I flew home to Louisville positively giddy.

Life in Louisville was busy and fun. Our growing, energetic boys leaned into soccer, gymnastics, bike riding, climbing trees and anything competitive. Everything became a contest in our house with them. "I can put my shoes on faster than you. I can drink my milk faster. I beat you to mommy."

Jay's job responsibilities quickly expanded beyond Louisville, and he began travels around the US and internationally. I joined him as often as I could, including memorable trips to Australia, New Zealand, Austria and more. I loved managing the kids, the household, my work, fun outings with friends, and always planning our next adventure.

From our house you could jump on miles of running trails in the parks. Jay and I both took full advantage of this resource. As often as his schedule allowed, we carved out a weekly date night, luckily securing our friend Megan as a standing Wednesday night babysitter. Jay named our date night BREAD. This stood for Bike or Run. Eat and Drink. We ran or mountain biked and ended up at an Irish pub called Molly Malones. He'd order a burger; I'd select a veggie burger and we would split a big basket of sweet potato fries. We'd usually have three pints, one for each of us and a third to split.

After what became busy school years, we spent our summers in Michigan. I was able to escape with the boys for eight-plus weeks to the cool, crisp Michigan weather and I relished doing the things Jay and I loved as kids - fishing, sailing, swimming, climbing sand dunes, building campfires, stargazing and spending time with family. I taught the boys how to sail, and they taught me how to release a sunfish and put a worm on properly. I chased them with sunscreen. They chased me with squirt guns. We spent endless days in Lake Michigan, jumping in the waves, body surfing and swimming out to the sand bar. At the end of the day, we snuggled close together, reading bedtime stories as our sandy feet intertwined in the crisp sheets. With one boy under each arm, I breathed in their damp hair. I had everything I ever wanted, right here.

There was so much joy.

KINDNESS MULTIPLIES

Sometimes, a simple kindness can change the world. In November 2007 I was focused on maintaining a healthy pregnancy, enduring cancer treatments, finishing the renovations on our home so we could move back in by Christmas, chasing after a toddler, and continuing to meet the demands of my job. I knew I was going to lose my hair, but I hadn't had time to do anything about it yet.

Then, one day a package arrived in the mail. As I cut open the tape on the cardboard box, brightly colored scarves overflowed from the package. On top of the colorful scarves was a small piece of paper that said, "You can do this."

I dug into the box, pulling out a colorful array of silk, cotton, and satin scarves - black and white, brown with magenta flowers, red, orange, purple. I held them in my hand, realizing the gift I had just discovered.

Kelley was a dear friend of my friend Alli. Alli had mentioned Kelley's story to me after my diagnosis. Kelley was diagnosed the previous year and had endured surgeries, toxic chemo, and the prognosis of losing her fertility. All this was incredibly overwhelming to me, having never met another young woman with cancer. But Alli's story ended with her doing well. She no longer needed these scarves so she wanted me to have them. I sent Kelley an email of appreciation, but frankly was a little too afraid to talk with her directly. I was cautiously entering this world of cancer.

Kelley's box of scarves sat prominently on my dresser as a reminder I would soon lose my hair. At first, I was scared of them, but I would touch them occasionally as I walked past the box. I was glad to know I had them when the time came that I needed them.

As my hair started to thin, I tried on Kelley's scarves and felt a growing sense of relief knowing another young woman had faced cancer and made it through to pass these brightly colored scarves on to me. On New Year's Eve, welcoming 2008, we shaved my head on our back deck. Our two-year-old son Wills caught my brown tufts of hair in the wind and blew them like a dandelion around the yard. His giggle helped me choke back my tears.

As I rubbed my hand over my bald scalp for the first time, I felt a sense of power. I took control of this hair loss. When so much seemed out of our control, this moment felt empowering, in a way I didn't expect.

Moments later, I searched through Kelley's box of scarves and found a white and black scarf to cover my small, newly bald head. We were going out with friends to celebrate New Year's Eve. Here I was, pregnant, newly bald, chemo fatigued, but wrapped in the hope a stranger had sent me. I felt beautiful and eagerly optimistic about what 2008 would hold.

To my surprise, I walked into our friend's home for a little New Year's Eve party and all my friends were wearing Kelley's scarves! Our mutual friend Alli had arranged with Jay to pick up the box of Kelley's scarves while we were at dinner and brought them to the party. My friends dug through the box finding the one they wanted to wear and put them on in solidarity before I arrived. Even some of the guys were wearing the scarves.

I walked into the party and laughed out loud at the ridiculousness of my amazing friends. Again, Kelley's scarves were a beautiful reminder of the power of connection and solidarity. We snapped a picture of them all holding me up in joyous celebration as we welcomed 2008 with hope and determination.

I wore Kelley's scarves throughout my treatment and collected many others as gifts from friends over the year I was in treatment. I never wore a wig because I felt more comfortable in scarves. As I healed and my buzz cut started growing in, I emailed Kelley for her address so I could return her scarves. She told me to just find someone else who could use them.

A month later, I traveled to a Young Survival Coalition Conference in Texas with my mom. I was excited to learn about living life after cancer and connecting with other young women who had been through what I endured the past year. I tucked a couple of Kelley's scarves in my suitcase hoping I might meet someone I could share them with as Kelley had so graciously done for me.

The second morning of the conference, my mom and I sat in the lobby looking through the day's agenda. I noticed two friends sitting nearby laughing together. One was fidgeting with an obviously uncomfortable wig. I pulled out Kelley's brown scarf with bright crimson flowers and walked over to the friends. I introduced myself and asked if I could join them.

I learned Roberta was newly diagnosed and her best friend Jen was by her side to help her navigate this scary new reality. I shared my story and what I had been through in the previous year. I held out the brown silk scarf and ran it through my fingers. I told them about how Kelley had sent it to me and how much it meant to me to wear it during my treatment knowing she had faced cancer before me. I asked Roberta if she would like it to wear as she faced what lay ahead for her.

She held the scarf in her hand, and we smiled with tears in our eyes. We were instantly connected by our shared story and this scarf. She pulled off her itchy wig and I showed her how to tie the scarf. We sat on the little wall beside the hotel plants and snapped a picture together. I hugged her and shared my contact information so we could keep in touch.

As I walked to our first session for the conference, I was moved by how much that scarf meant to me when I received it from Kelley when I was first diagnosed. I thought about how much I loved wearing it, as if it carried superpowers my other scarves didn't. And, then I realized how in this moment, how much it meant to give it away.

I passed along my strength and love and this soft, beautiful scarf to Roberta.

Instead of listening to the speaker, I immediately started dreaming about an idea to make this possible for thousands of women. My heart was exploding with ideas. Individuals could request a scarf for themselves, and we could have a gift scarf program where you requested a scarf for someone you know who is facing cancer. We could collaborate with hospitals and cancer support organizations to share scarves with their patients.

I knew the power of storytelling. I could help women reflect on their experiences and heal as they passed their scarves and story on to someone else. We could help newly diagnosed women feel less isolated and more beautiful with this simple gift of a scarf. I started sketching out the logo. It was a ribbon made of all the colors of female cancers - pink, teal, purple, blue.

Later that evening, my mom and I joined Roberta and Jen for dinner. Roberta was wearing the scarf. I shared my idea with the table. I was going to start a nonprofit organization, collecting scarves and stories from cancer survivors, and passing them on to others in treatment.

It would be called Hope Scarves.

HOPE SCARVES IS BORN

We had come to love our new home in Louisville, Kentucky. I played the song "Home is Wherever I'm With You" by Edward Sharp and the Magnetic Zeros repeatedly as we explored our new city. As we discovered parks, running trails, breakfast spots and music festivals, I decided I would stay home with our young boys instead of finding a job right away. I just wanted to slow down and be fully present with them. We had big adventures each day with art projects, trips to the zoo, soccer games, sidewalk chalk and sprinklers. Though I loved being with them, I came to realize I also missed my professional outlet of working in the non-profit sector. My idea for Hope Scarves kept percolating.

One day, Jay and I were sharing a beer on our patio as the kids splashed in the kiddie pool. I was expressing my desire to do something professionally part-time, and he said, "Well, why don't you start this organization you keep talking about?"

His sly smirk already knew the answer. Jay's gentle nudge was just what I needed to actually take the scary first step. I grabbed a fresh IPA and took my laptop up to the hammock in our backyard and pounded out my first business plan right then and there. I wrote frantically, trying to get all my ideas down on paper. I wrote how the scarves could be requested by patients or sent as gifts by loved ones. I brainstormed how we could partner with hospitals and cancer support organizations to share scarves where patients already went for support. As my ideas flowed, my excitement grew.

Though I had spent my entire career in the non-profit sector and had a master's degree in Public Administration, I had no idea how to turn an idea into an actual nonprofit. I signed up for a class at Louisville's Center for Nonprofit Excellence titled, "How to start a nonprofit." With a fresh notebook open to the first page, I eagerly awaited my instructions.

The first thing the instructor said was to do an extensive review of existing organizations to understand if anyone else was already providing the services planned for our new organization. Then he shared some scary statistics based on how many organizations don't last more than a year. I was excited, but nervous, at the end of the class. I went directly to a coffee shop to Google every possible way I could figure out if anyone was doing what I had in mind for Hope Scarves.

I typed with disappointment in my heart, thinking there must be an organization out there already doing this. It seemed like such an obvious idea. To my delight I couldn't find an organization that was pairing scarves and stories together and sharing them with cancer patients. There were lots of places to buy or get free scarves, but the story was what made Hope Scarves unique, and no one was doing this. My excitement grew. Next, I searched www.hopescarves.org as a domain name. It was available. I bought it on the spot.

I believed so strongly in the potential of Hope Scarves that once I understood the path, I couldn't help but run.

While the boys were in pre-school in the morning, I used those precious hours wisely. I would go to yoga then walk across the street to a little coffee shop where I tucked myself in the corner at a large round table, papers spread in various piles. I painstakingly completed the 1023 application with the IRS, and worked out the business model and funding structure. I created a board of directors, made up of friends and family from four different states. I wrote by-laws and articles of incorporation. Focusing on the logistics of starting a business was fulfilling and exhilarating. The dream of Hope Scarves took shape.

I had setbacks along the way. Paperwork I filed with the state of Kentucky needed correction so one sunny day in November, two-year-old Bennett and I went on a field trip to the capitol in Frankfort. We climbed the marble stairs and found our way to the correct office in a labyrinth of bureaucracy. Miraculously, I had brought the correct changes and my amendments were approved while Bennett snacked on Cheerios. Hopping down the steps together, I was so proud to be creating this organization with him by my side. We snapped a selfie on the steps of the capitol to commemorate one more step in the right direction for my dream.

As I worked through the administrative and logistical aspects of starting a business, what I came to realize was the power of turning heartbreak into hope. In creating Hope Scarves, I was also writing my own story. Cancer wasn't going to get the last word. It had taken so much from our young family, but our story didn't stop there. Hope Scarves was my personal way of writing a brave new chapter.

I could take my personal experiences and love for storytelling and create something beautiful for the world. In doing so, the feeling I had when I put on that first scarf from Kelley would be felt by thousands around the world. The energy I felt from this realization empowered me. I was still only a couple years out from my cancer treatment, but the idea of creating a community of storytellers sharing scarves was invigorating.

I went for trail runs and would stop dead in my tracks with plans. I'd pull my phone from my pocket to jot down an idea or a name of someone I wanted to be sure I shared the organization with. I was living in this new city, trying to make friends and find my people, teetering between cancer Lara and Lara living beyond cancer.

I realized Hope Scarves wasn't just a resource for other newly diagnosed people to receive scarves and stories, it was the community I was looking for. It was filling a void I had in my life. Hope Scarves would be a community of women connected by scarves and stories and a place for people to volunteer and be part of bringing love to the world.

I was creating my village.

Hope Scarves was born in the spare bedroom of our house with my two-year-old volunteer drawing pictures on printer paper under my desk. I slowly collected scarves and stories from cancer survivors, organizing them on hangers with corresponding cards in a recipe box to keep the story paired with the scarf. I built a website and launched a Facebook page. I felt the healing power of helping others.

I connected with young women in Louisville who were starting treatment, by bringing Hope Scarves to their homes. I told them about Kelley, myself, and Roberta and how the idea for Hope Scarves came to be. I showed them how to tie their scarf and explained that the story it carried was what made it so special.

As word of Hope Scarves grew on social media, scarf donations arrived in my mailbox with stories. Each time I received a package I squealed out loud. The notes that accompanied the stories reinforced the excitement for my dream. Women wrote about how they weren't sure what to do with their scarves after treatment and were so excited to find us. They shared how writing their story helped them reflect.

One of my favorite notes was when a woman from Pennsylvania described Hope Scarves as "a chain letter... only better." I recruited my friends to volunteer to help me package scarves and make bracelets out of scarves that didn't work in the Hope Scarves collection as a fundraiser. My village was growing. Hope Scarves was a door through which many people came into my life and each time I felt more fulfilled and connected.

In that first year, I had the opportunity to participate in a program called Ignite Louisville through The Leadership Louisville Center. It paired nonprofit organizations with teams of young professionals to solve problems and build capacity. The timing was perfect because suddenly, I had a team of people ready to help me through the program. The team of nine mostly men stuffed themselves into my second-floor spare bedroom office. Jay laughed as they walked one by one up to our first meeting. The most remarkable thing this group did was what I like to call stage an intervention.

One day they sat me down and explained that there were two ways for Hope Scarves to go. Both options were great, but only I could decide. Was Hope Scarves a small little project I did in my spare bedroom in between tennis matches and room parent responsibilities or was it a national nonprofit organization?

I didn't waste a moment in my answer, I passionately replied, "It is an international nonprofit organization with the potential to change the way people experience cancer."

I quit my tennis team that afternoon.

THE UNTHINKABLE MOMENT

Five years, six years, seven years since the cancer diagnosis, and time marched on and my healthy body carried me from one adventure to another. Our family was thriving in Louisville - Saturday mornings on the soccer field, house projects to update, the transitions between baby rooms to big-boy bedrooms, and trips to the Florida Keys to fish and snorkel.

On one trip south, we kayaked in the mangroves until we found a little cove with a rope swing. One by one, we each precariously climbed out of our kayaks onto the slippery roots of the mangroves to take our turn on the rope swing. We caught snapper on almost every cast and ate peanut butter and jelly sandwiches as flying fish jumped around us. I shared a kayak with Wills. Jay had Bennett in his.

I loved that they were little enough to squeeze into kayaks with us and that at such young ages we took them on big adventures. As we bobbed in the turquoise water of that hidden lagoon, I looked at our family; a healthy, happy, little crew, and understood that this is what I fought for. I was living my dream.

Hope Scarves continued to flourish. On February 12, 2012, Hope Scarves officially became a 501(c)3 non-profit organization. Friends continued to gather in our spare bedroom to help wrap scarves. I hired my first employee, Erica. Soon, 113 donated scarves became a part of the collection, and 62 survivors shared their cancer story. That year, we sent 84 Hope Scarves packages to women newly diagnosed with cancer.

During the summer, we held our very first event in the backyard of a friend's house. The event was to share my dream of Hope Scarves and to raise money to support its mission. We strung lights across the back patio, moved the furniture in her living room to hold a silent auction, and we served BBQ and beer to friends. It was casual, yet classy.

Despite some doubting friends, I charged people to come and learn about my little idea, and to my delight, not only did they come, but we raised $30,000 in one evening! Soon after, Hope Scarves moved into its first office space and became a thriving nonprofit in the Louisville community. By the end of 2013, nearly 600 scarves had been sent across the nation, building connection, love, and encouragement among cancer survivors.

In late 2013, I developed persistent low back pain. On our last stretch of a Christmas whirlwind visiting family throughout Michigan, we took the boys to Chicago to visit their Uncle Eric and see the Aquarium. The boys sat on the edge of their seat for the dolphin show and their eyes grew huge as the wall opened up behind the tank, revealing Lake Michigan as far as you could see. "It's like the dolphins are swimming in Lake Michigan, mommy!" Bennett giggled. I nodded in agreement but couldn't shake the intense pain in my low back from sitting on the auditorium's concrete seats. I put my coat under my tush, my hands, no matter how I tried I could not get comfortable. After the show we followed the crowd through the obligatory gift shop exit line. The boys each excitedly bought magnets with floating dolphins, and I snagged a travel pack of ibuprofen to ease my pain. On the ride home to Louisville the next day, I had to lay my chair as flat as possible to relieve the pressure in my lower back. Something was not right.

At the office the following week I did stretches on the floor of Hope Scarves with Erica, our Program Coordinator, who herself had low back pain. I went to my massage therapist, but only felt more excruciating pain upon leaving. Nothing brought me any relief. I contributed it to an excessive amount of time on my computer since I was working so much at Hope Scarves.

Or maybe I did too much trail running. Friends repeatedly reminded me, "We are getting older." Yes, that must be it. I called my doctor to discuss my concerns just to be safe. She agreed that given my health history it was worth looking into and ordered an MRI to get a closer look.

I hadn't had a scan other than a PET scan seven years earlier. Laying on the table, my mind wandered for the first time to the scary possibility of cancer. I always thought cancer would come back in my chest or lymph nodes. I hadn't thought much about it coming back in my bones. Surely that wasn't what was happening. I quickly dismissed this as a possibility and tossed the disc they gave me into my purse as I left.

We had tickets that night for our family to attend a University of Louisville basketball game. It was a "white out" for fan attire, so I wanted to pick up white UofL shirts for the boys as a surprise before the game. Later that afternoon, dressed all in white, Jay and I and two very excited little boys headed to the basketball game, but first, we made a quick stop to drop the MRI disc off to our good friend and neighbor, Cody, who is a radiologist and offered to read the scan for me.

I left it in his mailbox and jumped back in the car as a shooting pain ran up my back. I shook it off and joined in the excitement of the evening. We had a fun dinner across the street from the Yum! Stadium and walked in with thousands of other fans. The boys were pumped!

Our seats were a gift from a friend - box seats with plush, comfy chairs. I was relieved to have a cushion as my pelvis throbbed. The stadium was electric with excitement and the Cardinals were winning. Jay bought the boys a big tub of popcorn and drinks. Life didn't get any better.

At the start of the second quarter my phone rang. It was Teresa, Cody's wife. Why would she be calling me, she knew we were at the game? She was quiet. Slowly and calmly, in her doctor voice she said, "Lara, can you go somewhere quiet to talk?"

I looked across our two, popcorn-oil-faced little boys to Jay. Pointing to my phone I said, "This is Teresa, she wants to talk." I got up and made my way to a miraculously placed private bathroom right at the end of our section. I slipped inside and locked the door behind me.

She took a deep breath and explained that Cody reviewed the scan and even had another friend and neighbor come over and look at it with him to be sure. It looked like I had a large tumor in my sacrum.

She explained that our mutual friend Mike, an oncologist, was available to talk with me further.

I was in complete shock. "OK" I said. We said, "I love you" and hung up.

Thirty seconds later, Mike was on the other end of the phone. In the same calm, collected doctor voice, Mike explained that it looked like I had a large tumor in my sacrum. I thought to myself, I need to Google sacrum. He said they didn't know for certain if this was breast cancer, but the way it was presenting looked like that it was most likely.

Breast cancer? Sacrum? My head started spinning. I leaded against the dark grey wall and slowly sunk to the tiled floor, my legs pulled in close in front of me.

He continued, "If this was my wife, Ashley, I would get into an oncologist as soon as possible." He had already made a couple calls and a friend of his, Dr. Patrick Williams, was willing to come in early the next morning to meet with me before his first scheduled patient.

"OK," I said again, only half comprehending the words being spoken to me. I didn't have an oncologist in Kentucky. I hadn't even thought about needing one.

My phone buzzed again, and it was Teresa. "I'm so sorry Lara," she said. We talked for a minute, but I was in a daze. Here I was again, in a public bathroom, processing earth shattering news, as I had seven years earlier. Only now I was alone. There was no baby gently kicking my belly, no toddler checking on me. My life was out there cheering on the Cardinal basketball team, where everything was OK.

I pulled myself off the floor and held onto both sides of the sink, staring at myself in the mirror. How could this be happening, again? I couldn't get myself to walk out the door and into a world where I was again a cancer patient. How could I tell Jay? What would this do to our happy little family? What did this even mean?

And where exactly was my freaking sacrum?

RECLAIMING MY LIFE
DESPITE MBC

Eventually, I opened the door to the bathroom January 9th, 2014, and walked into a world where I was never the same. Gone was the peace of mind that cancer was behind us. In a flash, the comfort and strength we had wrapped ourselves in for "beating cancer" as a young family that led a healthy, full, life vanished. My reality of survivorship shattered into a million pieces.

I stood at the top of our row in the basketball stadium, looking out over the thousands of lives and then down at Jay and our two boys. I stood there for a while, just watching them. I didn't want to walk toward them with this news. Wills was in 3rd grade, Bennett in kindergarten. Though they were bigger than the first time I was diagnosed, they were still so young.

I slowly made my way down the red stairs to our section. Jay looked up at me, expectantly. I just shook my head, tried to hide my tears, and whispered, "It's not good. Let's talk about it later." I grabbed his hand behind the boys, squeezed it tightly, and added, "I just want to enjoy tonight."

Jay squeezed my hand, let go, and started cheering with the boys, "Let's go Cards!"

The next morning, we were in the oncology office by 8 A.M. Dr. Williams confirmed what our friends had thought by saying it looked like metastatic breast cancer (MBC). To be sure, he scheduled a biopsy for the next day, which confirmed the horrible set in motion a whirlwind of emotions and appointments.

Like many early-stage breast cancer patients, I avoided learning about MBC because it scared me. I preferred to avoid this reality as opposed to understanding it. As a result, I was unprepared and overwhelmed. After the appointment, I walked to the top of the parking deck, slowly sliding my hands along the dirty concrete. I needed fresh air. I needed to see the sunshine.

From the top of the parking deck I reckoned through tear-filled eyes that the world was still the same. The stop lights turned from red to green. A group of doctors hurriedly crossed the street. The highway buzzed in the distance. Yet, nothing about our reality seemed to make sense.

In an instant, we were plucked from our happy, healthy, disease-free survivorship and thrown back into the world of cancer.

I sat in my living room late that night, legs crossed on the couch by the glow of the laptop screen, absorbed in Google searches that took me down dark paths of despair. The average life expectancy was 2-3 years. About 114 people die every day of MBC in the US. Thirty percent of early-stage breast cancer patients go on to develop metastatic breast cancer. MBC is the leading cause of death for women under 50 years old. The statistics were terrifying.

I was outraged that no one was making a bigger deal of this reality for women. I sat there in shock at how victorious I had felt having "beat" breast cancer when all of this was right around the corner. I felt uninformed about the broader scope of the disease, and this made me angry. Why was I not given more information? Where was the outrage in the breast cancer world when so many women were dying of metastatic breast cancer? How was it possible that I could count in the "98% survival at five years" statistic only to become metastatic two years later, and not be counted? My questions fueled my confusion and rage.

At the same time, I felt relieved that I hadn't lived bound by the fear of recurrence. I didn't have a single regret with how we had spent the past seven years of "cancer-free survivorship." I loved how strong and healthy and hopeful I felt with cancer behind me. I was grateful I didn't consume myself with the fear of recurrence. I loved the joy of beating cancer. I loved the strength I felt making it through breast cancer.

Balancing these conflicting feelings was confusing.

The most surprising part of the shifting from an early-stage breast cancer patient to a Stage 4 patient was that there was no set treatment path. When I was diagnosed with Stage 2, there was a treatment plan and a light at the end of the tunnel. I was given a "welcome bag" and supported by a nurse navigator. There were support groups and women reaching out to me to share their survivorship stories. When I walked out of the cancer center on the morning of January 9th, 2014, I walked into an unknown, dark, terrifying world of Stage 4, metastatic cancer. I was horrified and alone.

My new doctor explained that the cancer was still highly estrogen driven and that was a good sign. Finally, I thought, some kind of reassuring news! We decided I would have radiation treatment on the tumor to relieve my pain and shrink the tumor. I also decided to have my ovaries removed to dramatically reduce the amount of estrogen feeding the cancer.

I consulted with Dr. Harvey, the doctor who had seen me through my early-stage treatment in Birmingham. We talked on the phone, his warm, calm voice assuring me with his southern charm that there were many treatment options for me and that he had many patients living long, full lives with MBC. I tried to believe him, but my heart was breaking.

Desperate to be sure we were on the right path, on a cold, grey February day we traveled to Nashville, Tennessee, to meet with a highly recommended oncologist at Vanderbilt for a third opinion. We sat in the sterile office, eager to be reassured by a third doctor that I had reason to be hopeful.

Instead, a recognized "expert oncologist" in her field took out a pad of paper and explained how metastatic breast cancer progressed. She wrote out the name of a drug and then drew a big black X over it. Explaining that it would stop working, then she drew another drug and a big black X, and another and another. She coldly said, "Each time a drug fails, you can expect less time on the following drug."

Right there in her office she outlined my demise in black Sharpie pen and crushed my budding hope. I walked out in a trance, confused that she could be so negative when the other doctors were encouraging. I called Dr. Harvey from the parking lot. He said,

"Listen Lara, you get me her name and in one year, you and I are coming back here and walking into her office and showing her how wrong she was."

The truth was what she said wasn't that different from the other doctors. It was the perspective in which they shared the news. An oncologist at the University of Louisville, Dr. Beth Riley, who ultimately would become my primary oncologist in Louisville, Dr. Harvey, and Dr. Williams all shared the same information as Dr. Heartless (not her real name) in Nashville. They just took a different approach.

Instead, they said, "You will stay on this drug as long as it works and hopefully that will be for a long time." They left room for HOPE. They didn't make promises, but they didn't take away the chance for things to go well. This experience showed me how important words are and how critical it is for doctors to understand the power in their words.

Weighing all these perspectives, I slowly tried to make sense of this new reality of MBC. Unable to sleep, I would wake up in the middle of the night and walk around my neighborhood for hours. I walked and cried and thought about my crumbling life. One day I was walking and crying at the moment the birds began to sing. I was rounding a hill in my neighborhood as the dawn light started to brighten the darkness when the silence changed to song. I stopped walking and listened.

Tears streamed down my face as I took in this moment of a new day. I sat on the curb of the narrow neighborhood street and sobbed with my hands on my head, deep, ugly cries. My pelvis was still healing from radiation, and I shifted uncomfortably on the concrete curb. I sat there crying until the sun shined brightly on a new day.

Slowly, slowly I started to piece together who I was. Again.

I was no longer the strong, victorious cancer survivor. I understood I had to become another version of myself. As much as I loved the healthy Hope Scarves founder, cancer survivor, example of survivorship and strength, I was now an MBC patient. This was my reality.

As the radiation healed and the pain subsided in my pelvis, I was desperate to control my circumstance. I read radical books about remission and diets, and I grasped onto clean eating. I changed everything about the way I ate. I cut out sugar, carbs, meat, and alcohol. I lost 20 pounds and my smile. I was desperate for something I could control to make myself healthy.

Four months into this diagnosis, extreme diet, and adjustment to living with MBC, we traveled to one of our favorite places in the Florida Keys for spring break. I packed my blender and stocked our condo with leafy greens. I hadn't yet found the ease of smiling. My shoulders were tense with fear. My laugh was distant. My heart, still broken, but we wanted to escape and try to enjoy time together as a family in a place we loved.

The first evening, Jay was fishing with the boys. The evening sunshine shimmered on the bay in front of our condo. The boys were running back and forth between their fishing poles. I looked out at them from our patio with love and awe of their easy joy. As I took a deep breath of the salty air, I thought what I really want is a bag of lime chips, salsa, and a cold Corona. I filled a cooler with these exact treats and walked down to Jay and my boys. I handed him a cold Corona and pushed two limes into the bottles.

He stared at me, questioning my judgment. "Cheers," I said.

From that sunlit moment, I created what I came to call a "joy filter." In each situation, I would ask myself, will this bring me joy? Sometimes a giant green smoothie brought me joy. Other times, it was a plate of sweet potato fries. I followed the idea of everything in moderation, even moderation, and I allowed myself to make choices that uniquely fit me. Joy was my guide to the people I surrounded myself with, the way I spent my time, the clothes I wore, and beyond.

At my first follow up scan, five months after the MBC diagnosis, I was given the glorious news that there was no progression. There were still signs of healing in my sacrum, but no active cancer. I learned a term I would come to love – NED – which meant "no evidence of disease."

With this wind in my sails, I started to think, OK, I may not be able to be cured, but can I heal? What does healing look like? How do

I make myself well and strong again, even with a terminal, Stage 4 diagnosis? I didn't need a book to tell me how to live my best was up to me. I gave myself permission to decide what this looked like, and once I did, I was set free of the bonds of the disease. I didn't know what my future held, but I was going to do MBC my own way, just as I had done with early-stage cancer and survivorship.

I was fortunate that the cancer responded to the removal of my ovaries and first line endocrine therapy. For the next five years I lived scan to scan. Each scan was a celebration that the cancer was not progressing. I was dancing with NED. Sometimes I was in the lead, other times the disease, but I learned how to live well with a terminal illness. I realized I wasn't dying tomorrow or most likely next week or next month.

And, I learned to live, not just be alive, but truly live.

I felt an immense need to pack in as much living into these healthy years as possible. The MBC diagnosis made our life more urgent and more precious. We traveled every chance we got. I have always loved to travel, but when I became metastatic it took on a new meaning. I often explained there was no room for cancer in my carry on. That was true. When I left on a trip I didn't take cancer with us. I left it all at home and released myself from the worry that nagged in the background, even when life appeared happy.

One morning at Toast, a favorite little breakfast place for our family, we made The Team Mac Adventure Manifesto in crayons on the back of a kids' menu. We went around the table, taking turns adding places to the list with five-year-old Bennett and eight-year-old Wills. Our list was ambitious: Disney World, RV trip, the Grand Canyon, a tropical island, an African safari and much more. We dreamed big.

And, in the intense way we approached any challenge, we got on it. The year I turned 40 was the most exciting year of my MBC living life tour. Our family swam with sharks in Belize, skied from the top peak in Big Sky Montana, and spent the summer in Michigan. I went to Mexico with college friends, and hiked the Red Rocks of Sedona, Arizona with my high school best friend. Jay and I went on a trip, just the two of us, to embrace the fresh ocean air of Big Sur, California.

While other people dread their 40th birthday, I was elated to have reached this milestone. I had ten years of facing cancer in my corner. Even after the progression, here I was, still living life with gusto! For my actual birthday, Jay and my friends planned a surprise party for me. Of course, I figured it out in the days leading up to it. As the social planner for the family, there were several signs, but I went along with it.

As Jay led me through Bluegrass Brewing Company that Saturday night, I squeezed his hand knowing there was something more in store. He led me to a set of stairs, up to a private event space. I skipped up the stairs. He looked back at me and said, "You know!"

"Yeah, and I can't wait!" I exclaimed.

He shook his head, laughed, and pulled back a thick velvet curtain.

"Surprise!" "Happy Birthday!" yelled a crowd of people. A live jazz musician played in the corner. Everyone was laughing. I was amazed at the people who came to celebrate with me, including high school friends, college pals, Alabama friends, Louisville friends, soccer moms, and the Hope Scarves community. It was all the people I loved in one room, and I was there, living and loving and celebrating life.

I went from being unable to walk at the height of the sacrum tumor pain, to running marathons and triathlons, climbing mountains, and repelling down waterfalls. I didn't take my health for granted. Each run started with a silent prayer of gratitude. I felt each breath and pounding heartbeat as a reminder of how precious health was. I lived each day with joy in my heart, cancer in my bones, and hope in my spirit.

Through the precarious practice of living well with a terminal illness, I came to understand that I could hold both fear and joy in the same hand, at the same time.

I wasn't living because I had "beat" cancer as I did before, I was living life over cancer, one day at a time. My joy and love didn't come through the solution to the problem. It was there, in the midst of the struggle. As was the pain. I was living and loving life, not because I was cured, but because I accepted my life as it was and found a way to be joyful regardless of my circumstances.

This became the definition of what I started calling My Hopeful Life - letting go of what you thought your life was going to be, and embracing the joy, sadness, pain and love that it is today. A Hopeful Life isn't a life absent of trauma and pain. It is a life that accepts struggle is part of the story, and, has hope regardless of what comes next.

TEN YEARS ON...

As I write this ten years from the founding of my nonprofit dream, Hope Scarves is indeed an international nonprofit organization. We've sent nearly 30,000 Hope Scarves to every state and 34 countries. We have partnerships with more than 55 hospitals in 22 states where Hope Scarves are shared directly with patients as part of their care. The oldest scarf recipient is 97 and the youngest just six months old. We support people facing over 90 types of cancer. Our staff of six and hundreds of volunteers busily sort scarf donations and send hundreds of Hope Scarves around the globe each week.

Each Hope Scarf still carries the same simple message of love that I felt when I received those first scarves from Kelley. It's simple, intentionally. Hope Scarves exists on the premise that recognizing how a small act of kindness will create something lasting and good for the world.

I am often asked, "Did you ever imagine Hope Scarves would be this big?"

I look them firmly in the eye and say, "I did."

It's been amazing to see my vision come to life each day and to watch it grow beyond my personal story. While much has remained true to my original vision, one important part of our work evolved over the past ten years.

When I became metastatic in 2014, we reflected on the work of Hope Scarves. The stories are inspiring, and the scarves are a practical resource during cancer treatment, but they aren't going to save anyone's life. If we were truly going to live out our vision of "To change the way people experience cancer" we had to do more.

As I faced the reality of a Stage 4 breast cancer diagnosis, I was enraged to learn how little of the billions of dollars raised for breast cancer went to Stage 4 breast cancer research. Immediately, I started working on a plan to expand the work of Hope Scarves. Our mission at the time was to "Support people facing cancer through scarves and stories of hope." With a quick edit of this sentence, we modified our mission to "Support people facing cancer through scarves, stories, and hope." Hope was not tied just to the story, but to research. Later, we went even further to clearly define our mission as it remains today - "Support people facing cancer through scarves, stories, and research."

I realized that for some women, like me, cancer isn't a one and done kind of gig. I will be in treatment for the rest of my life. Not everyone beats cancer, some live with it. Some die. I didn't want to share this part of the story before because I was so focused on hope.

I realized now you can focus on hope, but also acknowledge that hope comes in many forms. At Hope Scarves we have the incredible honor of sharing stories from many perspectives. Those "lifers" who face metastatic breast cancer are some of the most hopeful women of all.

Don't get me wrong, I love to celebrate. My friends know that PET scans and champagne go hand and hand. However, when we hyper focus on celebrating survivors and beating cancer we unintentionally alienate those who aren't "winning." In fact, the focus on beating cancer has become such a prominent symbol for breast cancer that those dying of breast cancer feel alienated and forgotten.

They feel so strongly that the breast cancer movement doesn't represent them that they created their own ribbon. It is teal and blue with a small bit of pink in the center. I found it incredibly disturbing that the people suffering the most, enduring heart wrenching devastation and painful treatments as they face death feel isolated from the very movement that set out to help them.

They shouldn't feel forgotten - they should be at the heart of the movement - represented by the most brilliant, deepest pink of all. I had a vision that in addition to celebrating all the people who beat cancer, there will be a colossal shift to rallying around those dying. I liken it to the AIDS movement in the 1980s. During the early epidemic, 40,000 men were dying every year—people marched, made noise, and got the drugs to keep them alive. The community rallied around the dying, demanding more money for research to help them, and demanded people see the heart wrenching pain of the disease. They didn't just rally around the healthy people and show pictures of smiling people who beat AIDS - they focused on the weakest and the sickest and demanded research to help them.

I appreciate that pink ribbon items are purchased with good intentions, but I dream of a day when the breast cancer movement widens the spotlight beyond celebrating survivors and shines light on funding metastatic research. I dream of a day when women no longer die of this disease. Yet in the breast cancer world, with millions of dollars in donations, only 2% goes to metastatic research.

This must change.

Research rounded out our work in remarkable ways and helped me again turn the heartbreak of my Stage 4 diagnosis into hope. We founded the MBC Research Fund at Hope Scarves where 100% of funds go directly to research. Donors can give to this fund directly or they can give to our general fund. Since launching the MBC Research Fund in 2015, we have to date raised one million dollars. We continue daily to nurture this important fund.

Beyond the research fund, I also changed the way we talked about cancer at Hope Scarves. I no longer wanted to use "battle" words like "fighting" and "beating," or limit the joy of survivorship to those who had overcome cancer.

I was surviving every day. As someone living with Stage 4 disease, I would never beat this disease. Instead, we started using words like "facing cancer" and "living life over cancer." We combed through our website and print materials to be sure all of our language was inclusive of all stages of cancer, and I started talking about the full spectrum of the cancer experience.

It focuses on not just the victorious beating cancer story, but the story of living life over cancer. No matter the stage. One day at a time. Our mission has become clearer and our work more important.

Hope Scarves started from my personal experience receiving a box of scarves from Kelley and passing them on to Roberta. From there it has grown into a community of love and support that wraps around the world. It is a community that today surrounds me with hope and love.

We belong to each other in a million ways.

IT'S NOT ABOUT THE PINK.

I never embraced the pink, victorious metaphors, tiaras, or tutus as a breast cancer patient. However, I did fully love the idea of survivorship as I had come to understand it. There was something about crossing over a magical bridge from cancer patient to survivor and having faced down "the enemy", endured the treatments, surgeries, scans, and uncertainty to be crowned "cancer free." I felt like I emerged victorious with a greater perspective, gratitude, and willpower.

Facing early-stage breast cancer was a "battle." Being diagnosed at age 30 and seven months pregnant was earth shattering. Following treatment, I was depressed, overwhelmed, and struggling in a sea of PTSD. I worked through this with the help of a counselor, other early-stage survivors, and most of all the power of turning heartbreak into hope by starting the non-profit, Hope Scarves.

I remember walking out of my first follow up appointment, six months after the conclusion of treatment, and literally feeling like I was flying. When leaving the cancer center, you cross a window-lined sky bridge back to the main hospital. That day, it felt like it was a literal bridge back to life. The sun was shining, and rainbows danced across the floor guiding me back to the life I loved. I was going to live. Live. Live!!!! I would see our children grow up, and Jay and I would grow old together. I would get to hike the Grand Canyon and experience a safari in Africa. I allowed myself to dream again. I was no longer afraid of the future.

I beat cancer!

Throughout my early-stage treatments in 2008 there was a constant theme of hope. There was a light at the end of the tunnel, with everyone working toward my healing. We were supported and loved through surgeries, infusions, and scans. There was a clear enemy and a clear path to defeating it. While terrifying, it was also empowering. We could see the determination and willpower welling up in our young family. We were going to make it through. We could see the light we were all reaching towards.

Seven years later, I faced the worst fear of a cancer survivor. Reoccurrence. The cancer was back, this time metastatic, or that it spread from the original site to a distant location in the body. I was thrown into the terrifying unknown of metastatic disease. The early doctor appointments and conversations were much different than the first time around. There was no clear path, steps to recovery or light at the end of the tunnel. Instead, doctors talked about "slowing the spread," "holding off the disease," "trying one therapy until it failed and then trying another."

Words were more passive than the aggressive treatment plan in the early stage. Instead of climbing toward a goal of survivorship, this time it felt like slipping slowly toward my death. While I was clinging to science, research, and a drug that might work, all I felt was falling toward my impending death.

I was not prepared for this huge shift in cancer care. When I was thrown back into the world of cancer, I thought I would be prepared. I had done this before, and though I almost puked in a trash can walking back into the cancer center, I knew I could face this again.

But this time, everything felt different. From the beginning of treatment, I was falling.

I found ledges of safety and stability at times. Some of those perceived ledges were even large and secure with a place for me to set up camp and comfortably stay for years. But I looked around and saw others falling constantly. Not many had the same stability I "enjoyed", so I knew my ledge could crumble at any time.

So often people just didn't understand my diagnosis. They weren't sure if I was cured, or sick, or why I was running half-marathons but talking about having a terminal cancer diagnosis.

"At least people will stop saying, 'But you don't look sick,'" were the first words I muttered in the exam room when, after seven years of treatment, my doctor explained that oral endocrine therapy drugs would no longer work. I was left with only IV chemo options and would lose my hair.

Many people didn't understand what I was facing. Many still don't.

It's not their fault. For the past 30 years, breast cancer has become a huge pink machine, raising billions of dollars and awareness. Having grown up amid all the pinkness I had a self-breast exam guide hanging in my sorority house bathroom. I ran the Komen 5K runs and celebrated survivors right along with everyone else. It felt good to see so many women surviving breast cancer.

It wasn't until I became metastatic that I realized how short sighted the messaging was.

I didn't feel like I fit into the narrative of the pink celebration any longer. I had the pink boxing gloves and the will to win, but I would never "beat cancer." That is the reality of Stage 4 metastatic disease.

I was frequently asked to speak at or attend breast cancer survivor luncheons in October. They often start with the emcee asking all the breast cancer survivors to stand up and stay standing depending on how long they have survived - 1 year, 5 years, 10 years, 20 years, until one sweet little old lady is standing having survived breast cancer for 47 years. Everyone cheers, and she often gets a gift basket filled with assorted pink items.

One year, I asked my MBC friend Robin to join me at one of the luncheons. She was weak from her chemo, but always eager to get out and about. I knew she had experienced progression recently and was not feeling well that night. She stood with everyone else, balancing herself on the back of her chair. She quietly sat down before the five-year survivorship was announced. Her eyes cast downward as she tugged on her purple scarf. Then she kindly applauded as the celebration continued to honor the last remaining woman standing.

I was infuriated watching Robin and looking around the room at the celebration.

The last woman standing, who was diagnosed with cancer 47 years ago, was lucky. Damn lucky. She deserved to be celebrated, but the reason she was alive is because the cancer in her body didn't metastasize or spread to other parts of her body. She endured treatments that back then were probably pretty rough, but she went on to live a long, healthy life.

I wanted so badly to grab the microphone from the emcee and tell them about Robin. I wanted to explain how hard it was to sit among this pink celebration and not be seen or understood. I wanted to celebrate the survivors, but then turn everyone's attention to the reality of what Robin and I faced as Stage 4 patients. Our path was never-ending treatments, scans, fear, anxiety, and death.

Why was no one talking about the whole spectrum of breast cancer? Was it because it was scary, too hard to accept, and didn't sell merchandise? The advocate inside me grew as I learned more about how little of the billions of dollars raised in the name of breast cancer were spent on Stage 4, MBC research for those of us actively dying. As I mentioned, nationwide, only about 2% of funds raised support Stage 4 MBC research. That is all. I didn't know why this was happening, but I had to figure out how to change it.

I started sharing my dream that the breast cancer movement celebrate survivors but prioritize love, attention, and financial resources on saving lives. Instead of Stage 4 MBC patients feeling so left out of the pink ribbon, why couldn't MBC patients be at the center of the pinkness? If even a fraction of the billions spent on awareness and detection was shifted to accelerating treatment options and extending lives of those living with MBC, everyone would win. What if breast cancer becomes a chronic disease you can live with through effective treatments?

With science and support I hope that MBC patients will feel less like they are falling off the cliff and more grounded in the hope that they can live life over cancer. One day at a time.

It is time to show the truth of this devastating diagnosis and not lead with the celebration.

And, always hope.

HOPE IS NOT CONTINGENT

As the metastatic breast cancer story goes, this dance with NED since 2014 didn't last forever. In 2018, I experienced the first MBC progression with a new tumor in my femur. I had been fearing this moment for so long that it was almost a relief when it happened, and I didn't drop dead. I was actually in the airport flying to a high school friend's wedding in Michigan. My oncologist called to tell me the news.

It was the first time in four years the scan didn't provide us good news. I sat staring out the big window of the airport Starbucks, writing down the details she shared with me. I called and talked to Jay. In tears, he asked if he should come to the airport and get me. No, I said. The whole point of this struggle is to keep living. I was getting on that plane. I was going to this wedding and I was not going to stop living!

After I returned, we addressed this new tumor with more radiation. I stayed on the oral medication that seemed to be working for the most part. This progression helped me understand the "chess match" of treating MBC. There are multiple options, and you make a choice that will bring you stability but also maintain your quality of life. At this point, I felt my quality of life was pretty great. I was training for a half-marathon, working full-time, running around with my kids, practicing yoga, and of course checking off items on the Team Mac Adventure Manifesto.

I didn't feel sick.

Unfortunately, three months later the next scan showed additional progression. I had suspicious fluid in the lining of my left lung. My doctor recommended a thoracentesis to drain it and examine the fluid. She got me in the next day for the procedure.

That evening I ran three hard, fast miles on the treadmill. Fluid in my lung? I'll be damned. My breath was my strength, a grounding source of energy and a powerful advantage in my running. My breath was my calming source of peace in my mediation practice.

That following afternoon, I sat anxiously watching our boys' holiday program. I soaked up the love and joy of the season and snuck a little wave to 2nd grade Bennett as he made his way up to the risers to sing. I wrapped them in hugs following their program and passed them off to friends who I had arranged to spend the afternoon with while I had this procedure.

I drove myself to the hospital and checked in for the procedure. After I was prepped, I laid in the stiff hospital bed, waiting for my turn. It was days before Christmas, and I had a long list of errands and projects I would rather do than lay in a bed in the basement of the hospital. I twisted the sheets into knots, waiting for the procedure. I couldn't shake thinking that how days before my biggest concern was that I still hadn't decorated our pots with Christmas greens.

They wheeled me back for the thoracentesis. I had no idea what to expect. They sat me on the edge of the gurney, leaning over a pillow on another bed. The interventional radiologist used an ultrasound on my back to assess the situation. A sensitive nurse held my shaking hands. Then, the doctor started to laugh. Confused, the nurse and I looked back at him.

"I don't see any fluid," he remarked. "I wouldn't know where I'd even start a drain. There is literally nothing to drain."

As he cleaned up the ultrasound gel from my back, I looked at the nurse, and asked, "Is this a Christmas miracle?"

We both started crying. As they wheeled me back to the prep area, I was crying and laughing in that hysterical way you do when emotions are pounding through you too fast to process. I was shaking from head-to-toe with relief, excitement, and nervous joy. The nurse pulled the curtain closed on my hospital bay with a big smile and said, "I guess you get dressed and head home."

As soon as that curtain slid along the metal track, I pulled my clothes out of the big plastic hospital bag and got dressed. I couldn't stop smiling and squealing with excitement. Pulling back the curtain, I practically ran out of the hospital, stopping to hug a couple nurses as I squealed in joy.

I stopped at the registration desk and exclaimed, "There is no fluid! No fluid!"

I called my doctor from the car, but she wasn't as enthusiastic about my miracle hypothesis. Concerned the fluid would come and go, she said we had to keep an eye on it. I said, "OK, but can we agree that today there is not any fluid. And for that, we can be very happy?"

She paused. "Of course."

That was all I needed. It was my Christmas miracle, the most hopeful Christmas ever. Full speed ahead!

Jay was returning home from a business trip, and I couldn't wait to explain the roller coaster of a day I had! On my way home, I pulled over in a parking lot and recorded a live video to share with our friends and family on social media. I just needed to share this incredibly exciting news with everyone who loved us and who we loved. That year we hosted both sides of our family at our farm for Christmas. Every smile, gift, and meal was more special knowing how different it could have been with news of cancer progression.

Three months later, in March 2019, scans showed the fluid was back. Even though this news was devastating, it didn't take away from the magic of our Christmas miracle or the carefree, joyful times we shared in the bliss of the disappearing fluid.

The next thoracentesis did draw fluid from my lung, which was analyzed for cancer. As the roller coaster of MBC goes, my oncologist called a couple days later while I was having lunch with a couple of Hope Scarves board members working on partnership ideas. She explained that the analysis is often inconclusive because of the way they spin down the fluid to analyze the cancer.

They didn't find any cancer. She was again quick to explain that this doesn't mean there isn't cancer in the fluid. Again, I said, "But from what you saw today, you don't see any cancer?"

She answered, "Correct."

I clarified that I could be joyful in this news because that was all we had to go on at that moment. I hung up the phone and immediately ordered a bottle of champagne to round out our lunch with a toast to "Riding the MBC roller coaster."

Unfortunately, the fluid became a pesky nuisance I haven't been free of since then. At first it didn't cause me any issues, and I actually ran Hope Scarves' fundraising "Outrunning Cancer" half marathon with our team in the spring of 2019 with my left lung full of fluid. My other lung was so strong that it didn't cause me symptoms.

Days before our spring break trip to Costa Rica, another scan showed increased fluid, so I switched treatment to an oral drug called Ibrance. I was still not experiencing symptoms, so we didn't address the fluid with a drain. In Costa Rica, I surfed, ran on the beach, hiked up waterfalls and ziplined. There was no room for cancer in my carry-on! This treatment decreased the fluid through several scans. We were cautiously optimistic that we had found stability on this drug, just as we had with my five-year run on Arimidex.

Everything seemed to be going well for us. This drug was easily tolerated, Hope Scarves was embarking on a three-year strategic plan, and I launched My Hopeful Life, an extension to Hope Scarves. The kids were thriving in 6th and 9th grade. We had found our way to navigate the unpredictability of MBC. It wasn't easy, but each time things seemed unstable, we found our way through. I was strong, healthy and confident in my body.

Then, with the rest of the world, we were thrown the curve ball we never expected, COVID-19. To be safe in this scary new world of the pandemic, we moved our family of four to our holiday farmhouse in the countryside to get out of the city and ride out the unknown. We thought we'd stay a week, maybe two.

As the weeks added up, we settled into virtual work and school and life on the farm. While so much was unsettled in the world, we felt safe and grateful for our little "COVID cocoon." I woke up most mornings and hiked to the top of the ridge to write. We raced each other on a two-mile loop around the fields. We got baby chicks, built a chicken coop, planted gardens, and even adopted a little chocolate lab puppy. We took turns cooking meals and ate together every night. Even though it was a stressful time, and we missed our friends and family, I knew it was a sacred time for our family.

As the months went on, I had a harder time completing our two -mile loop. I figured I was just out of shape like everyone else cooped up in their homes during COVID. One day during a virtual yoga class, I had a hard time arching my back in wheel pose. My stomach muscles felt too tight to do a move I had done hundreds of times.

We hadn't left the farm for the city in weeks, but it was time for my monthly cancer treatment and scans. So, Jay and I left the safety of our farm in the early morning moonlight and drove back to the city. It was eerily quiet on the highway as we drove to the cancer center. The building, usually bustling with people, was almost empty. Masked and socially distancing, we waited for our appointment and scans.

We finished the scans and drove back to the boys on the farm. We walked our little puppy Cora and her eager, fluffy sister, Keeper, around the trails in the fields, which was our evening routine. I was slightly nervous about the scan results because of my breathing concerns, but I also felt confident this could be explained by the excess eating and lounging we'd done the past months.

Dr. Riley called the next day and quickly explained there was a dramatic increase in the fluid in my left lung. It was enough to believe the current treatment was no longer working. She recommended I switch to an oral chemo called Xeloda. We traveled back into the city a couple days later to drain the fluid again.

Switching treatment to an oral chemo made me more nervous and vulnerable to COVID. In late May, we moved back home to Louisville from the farm. I was not the healthy, strong woman who had gone into lockdown. I was filled with anxiety about cancer progression and terrified of contracting COVID in my already compromised lungs. It was a weird time around the world. Balancing progressing cancer and COVID was truly overwhelming. I had to dig extra deep to find peace and hope.

I reached back to the lessons I discovered when first diagnosed with metastatic breast cancer. I grounded myself in today and didn't live in the perceived future. I limited information on COVID trends and statistics, recognizing there was a fine line between being informed and being overwhelmed. And, I reminded myself that I knew how to hold both fear and joy in the same hand, at the same time. It was just that now...there was a lot more fear.

But I knew there was joy there, too.

Slowly, I found my way again.

I learned how to live after being diagnosed with Stage 2 breast cancer while pregnant.

I learned how to live after metastatic breast cancer.

And, I learned how to live with progression, even during a global pandemic.

I surrounded myself with people I loved, safely socially distanced, of course. In June, we packed up and went to Michigan, where we could safely create a cocoon of close friends and family and surround ourselves with things that brought us joy. We sailed, swam, climbed sand dunes, surfed, fished, and lived life with immense joy and gratitude.

Our summers in Michigan were a blessing every year. This year it brought incredible healing and strength. I absorbed each sunset into the core of my being. One day I paddled far out into the great lake, the waves slowly calming to a ripple. I laid down on my paddle board, my arms spread straight out on each side, fingertips dancing on the soft surface of the water.

I closed my eyes and took a deep breath. The warm sun eased the pain in my low back. I laid there for hours, drifting on the gentle current, thinking and dreaming and reflecting on my crazy roller coaster of a life.

When I got too hot, I rolled off the right side of my board, paddle in hand and sunk deep into the cold, refreshing water. I came up with a deep gasp, climbed back on my board and started paddling back to our cottage. I didn't know what the future held. I didn't know what the cancer would do next. But I knew I was living. I was strong. I was filled with love, and I had today.

As I neared our stretch of beach, I saw our boys laughing and throwing the frisbee. Wills dove for a catch, splashing into the cold water. Bennett laughed at his near miss. I smiled, gratitude radiating like the sun on this brilliant summer day. I had so much to live for. I had so much love.

I promised myself to live life one day at a time. Making the most of this one, precious life.

Regardless of what came next.

RIDING THE WAVES OF METASTATIC BREAST CANCER

BY LARA MACGREGOR

Some days are sunshine and sailboat rides
Others are torturous hours in a hospital basement
in a bone scan machine

Laying in the cold hard scan tube

I close my eyes and picture the seagull soaring above my head.
I wiggle my hands and tuck them into the sand.
I smell the dune grass
I hear the lapping of the waves
I feel a cool Lake Michigan breeze on my cheeks

I float away
Peaceful, calm, safe

Arms spread out wide, fingertips dancing on the waves...

I am free. I am alive.

With a startling jolt,
My eyes open to the scan machine an inch from my nose.

Deep breaths remind me of the invincible summer inside.
Wild and free.
Laughter and love radiate like the sun
even as the tears stream down my face.

And the bone scan buzz replaces the gentle sound of the waves
guiding me to freedom.

Live in the present · not the perceived future

Turn heartbreak into hope

LIVING AND GRIEVING

What is taken from us
while we are living is the saddest part.

We built this beautiful life, family, business,
friendships, hopes, and dreams. For years I said,
"We've been facing cancer since 2007 and there has been
more laughter than tears."

Despite all that we experienced, we found a way to endure. We found a way to keep going and living despite the roller coaster of good and bad news. We learned to hold both fear and joy in the same hand, at the same time.

But, when I entered the advanced stages of cancer and my body started failing, life as I knew it slipped away and what was left didn't feel like me at all. It made it hard to keep living when I was a shadow of the person I truly am.

There is this shared parenting idea that you never realize it's the last time your son grabs your hand to cross the street or calls you mommy or asks for one more story. We just think this will go on forever and then before we know it, no one is grabbing our hand to cross the street.

That's how I felt facing Stage 4, metastatic breast cancer. I didn't know I was running my last run. I didn't know I was climbing my last mountain. I didn't know I was dancing my last dance or jumping into the lake for the last time. I didn't know it was my last yoga class. My last deep, healing breath. I didn't know.

And now, I sit with all this loss. I am living, but grieving.

Grief is love. David Kessler explains, "The severity of grief is directly proportional to the amount of love." I guess this is why I am so sad. I am loved immensely. I love deeply. I love my life. I love the future I imagine for our family. I imagine walking out on the field with Wills for senior night. Seeing Bennett through high school. Taking trips together as a family, even as the kids wish they were with their friends. Visiting colleges. Tagging along on work trips with Jay. Being empty nesters with Jay! Finally spending all the money we've so diligently been saving. I see the cottage we bought. I see the trip to Africa. I fantasize about living on a sailboat in the Caribbean.

I am grieving the loss of the life we loved. I am grieving the future I thought I had.

Cancer ripped it away from me. It happened slowly at first, one by one, losing parts of me. My hair, my breasts, my ovaries, my carefree outlook on life all became victims. I found a way to rebuild myself without these things and I was still me. Despite all these obstacles, I ran five half marathons in Nashville and Louisville; I climbed mountains in Hawaii; I repelled down waterfalls in Costa Rica. I dove into an ice-cold lake in the Grand Tetons. I teetered on the edge of a cliff in Maine, encouraging our family to keep going when the trail seemed too dangerous. I showed my kids and nieces and nephew how to bravely swim with sharks in the Bahamas. I was strong and capable and full of life.

I loved and lived my life fully.

I learned not to live in the perceived future but ground myself in today. I remember the day my counselor proposed this idea to me. I wrote it down and circled it three times in my journal.

DO NOT LIVE IN THE PERCEIVED FUTURE. GROUND YOURSELF IN TODAY.

It was as if I was given permission to let go of the fears that bound me and more clearly see what was right in front of me. I didn't see my boys crying at my funeral. I saw them running in front of me on the soccer field. I stopped thinking about how much pain I would cause them in dying and started thinking about how much joy I could create today. I stopped wondering how the progression would go and what it would feel like to get sick from cancer and instead, started feeling the strength of my legs in yoga class and listening to my strong deep breaths as I ran the trails in Cherokee Park. I didn't sit on the shore of Lake Michigan and wonder if this would be my last summer. I tore off my cover up and dove into the freezing water, feeling fully alive and well on this day - the day I was living, right then.

In living intentionally each day I laugh more loudly. I hang onto hugs a second or two longer. If a song comes on that I like, I dance. I never let a moment pass to tell someone, "I love you" or "I appreciate you" or acknowledge the difference they make in my life. I light candles and buy plants. I drink only good wine.

I let go of things that once brought me down, like my body not being perfect, or comparing myself to others. I also became increasingly aware of the gift of growing older. I've always loved birthdays, but I took it up a notch, celebrating friends' birthdays in big ways and helping them see how special it was to grow older. I celebrated my 44th birthday with circus training by taking my friends to a class to learn silks, trapeze, and rings. We followed that with champagne and appetizers and so much laughter. Growing older deserves to be celebrated, not regretted.

When I was first diagnosed as metastatic, I was given an award as a "Pink Power Mom" and flew with our family to a gala in Atlanta. I was weak and full of nerves, still adjusting to the new reality of Stage 4 cancer. There I met Mary Ann. She had Stage 4 breast cancer. I watched her from a distance, laughing, drinking wine, telling jokes. I thought, "Why is she so happy? Doesn't she know she is dying?"

When she was finally not surrounded by people, I walked up to her and introduced myself, explaining I had recently been diagnosed with Stage 4 breast cancer. She hugged me so tightly, pulled me in front of her with both hands on my shoulders and asked about my family. We chatted for a little while about our kids. Then, she grabbed both my hands, holding them tightly in hers and with her beautiful smile and calming voice she brought her head close to mine and looked me in the eyes.

She asked, "If you had five minutes to live would you spend a second being sad?"

I thought, well, yeah, maybe a second or two, but I got her point. She was choosing life over fear. Her life was filled with joy and happiness, not because she was denying the reality of her diagnosis, but because she chose to live fully as long as she could.

Mary Ann died the following year, but more than that, I know she lived every second of every day that she had. I can still feel her hands holding tightly to mine, encouraging me to do the same. I didn't know it was possible that night, but I found a way.

I realized it was not just about staying alive, but to truly live, and I'm so glad I did.

I truly did. I lived for seven years, even with the roller coaster of Stage 4 breast cancer.

The perspective to be present and soak up each day with gratitude didn't come easily. It took hours of counseling, journaling, and reflection. Some days I fell into the worry of progression, living scan to scan with metastatic breast cancer. But, through hard work I found a way to live life more deeply, to treasure moments that others let slip by. I learned to laugh with my whole body and to live fully. I discovered how not to just be alive, but to truly live.

As I lived fully, I also carried a fear that the better I felt, the further I had to fall. Sometimes I would temper my wellness so as not to offend others with MBC who weren't as well as me. There were times when I was feeling great that people would say, "But, you don't look sick." While I appreciated and understood their compliment, I wished they knew how much mental gymnastics it took some days to live joyfully.

There were times I felt like I didn't want to be as happy as I felt because people would forget I had Stage 4 cancer. I was living well but not without the giant burden of Stage 4 cancer. The cancer wasn't gone, just controlled. I wanted my family and friends to understand that even when I was healthy and happy, I was carrying this burden. I needed them to remember this and to acknowledge my difficult reality. Also, I needed them to be ready, because I might need their help carrying this burden someday.

People often said, "You don't look sick."

Today, I look really sick.

The present isn't more reassuring than the perceived future, thanks to living with progressive, uncontrolled MBC, with weekly toxic treatments, crippling side effects and out of control disease. The present is terrifying, and I have no idea how much future is even possible.

I've even lost my treasured coping skill. I could no longer ground myself in today because today was just as agonizing as the perceived future. The only peace I found was in looking back at my life and finding gratitude in what I was once able to do. I completed a 70.3 Ironman Triathlon. I traveled the world. I chased my kids for hours in the park. I loved my husband fiercely. I treasured my family and friends.

I worked hard at living well with a terminal illness. I found a way to balance joy and sadness, anger and hope, dreams, and heartbreak. I learned how to live fully in the "and."

I believe there is no greater story than a life well loved. And, I love mine!

I found a way to live well with a terminal illness, but I am not sure how to decline well. What I am experiencing now in my weakness and pain is that life and death are mutually inseparable.

This is hard. I am struggling. How do I provide self-compassion when I don't even feel like myself? I used to say there is no room for cancer in my carry-on as I flew off an adventure. I also like to say there is no room for cancer on a boat, so I left my worries on the shore, even if only for a couple hours. But, here in this space I can't seem to step away from the burden. I can't put it down like I used to because it is 10 pounds of fluid filling my abdomen and making my back ache and my ankles swell. It is suffocating fluid crushing my lungs.

Today, I am still in treatment. It is a delicate balancing between hoping the toxic chemo will work and preparing myself for the reality that I have run out of options. Hopeful me thinks the chemo is working. I am sure that we are going to get good news soon and that scans will show that the cancer is shrinking and we will find a way to balance the toxicity to bring me more strength. I dream that there are still days ahead that will be filled with laughter and hope. But, I don't know if this is the right way to think? Would it be better if I focused on acceptance of my death?

Enlightenment comes when we accept. Accepting the heartache, the disease, the divorce, allows light in. It is a prick of light at first but then it grows stronger. Eternity is found in that moment of acceptance. Peace is found in acceptance.

I work on acceptance, but I just get mad. On a beautiful fall evening on our farm my family is running around playing in the golden sunshine. Jay is harvesting honey from our beehives. I am sitting on the deck, watching. It's something I never did before - I was always right in the mix. I try to take a deep breath and tell myself, be grateful for this moment.

Be grateful for this beautiful farm, for the sounds of laughter echoing in the rolling hills. Soak in the magic of this moment. But, instead of gratitude, I get angry. Why do I have to lose this? Why can't I keep living this amazing life? I am in disbelief. My life is so, so good. There is so much love. So much beauty. I have so many dreams and goals and plans. I can't find peace because I can't accept it. Not yet.

I learned how to live in the present instead of the perceived future, and I lived.

I pray that one day I will find acceptance and peace and die.

Today, I cry and put my hand on my heart, reminding myself, that even here. I am living.

Grieving and living. Living and grieving.

PMA:
POSITIVE MENTAL ATTITUDE

It was July of 2000 and Jay and I were adventure-seeking newlyweds on an Alaskan honeymoon. Our experiences included kayaking with whales from a remote cabin off the coast of Soldotna, salmon fishing in the Kenai River, and hiking up steep, sliding shale rock faces in bear country to find the best views of Denali. Our most recent stop was in the quirky town of Talkeetna, a basecamp for Denali climbs. We set up camp in a little campground at the end of the one lane road through town. As we did, an old, beat-up truck rolled by with a large fence secured with rope to the front of the hood. We learned later it was a bug catcher to protect the windshield.

The campground was a juxtaposition on life. Huge shiny campers, shut up tight to keep the air conditioning inside buzzed alongside wanderers and backpackers in rugged little tents and makeshift coverings, flapping in the summer breeze. Jay and I had a little backcountry tent, barely big enough for two people, with our gear stuffed in backpacks in the trunk or our rented Toyota.

It poured rain the first night we were there. The bright Alaskan sun glistened on our submerged tent as we groggily unzipped the fly and crawled out at a discouraging 5:00 AM. As we were drying out our soaked sleeping bags the door creaked open on the big tan and brown RV beside us. A dry, well-rested fellow stepped out, stretching his arms to take in the morning sunshine. This mustache-sporting chap, in his early 60's, physically fit and clearly happiest behind the wheel of his mammoth RV, strolled over to our drenched array of clothes and gear laid on the picnic table. The bright sun was shining through the poplar trees as he said, "Let me guess, pointing his steaming hot coffee cup in our direction, honeymooners?"

We smiled, "Yup!"

He sipped his coffee and said, "Do you want to know the secret to a happy marriage?"

We looked at each other as we rung out our socks and said, "Of course."

"PMA, he said, wisely, adding, "Positive Mental Attitude."

From then on, Jay and I engaged in PMA. From fixing the garage door I accidentally drove through on our new home, tiling a floor and not realizing you take out the spacers between the tiles before you grout, double-heading graduate school, training for marathons and triathlons, we certainly PMA'ed our way through life.

When Jay was given the opportunity to work overseas, we eagerly accepted. I resigned from my job at the United Way. We found a great flat and planned out our next two years in Liverpool, England. Then 9/11 happened and the world changed. His company scaled back their international program and instead, assigned him to Birmingham, Alabama.

I cried, disappointed to lose the international adventure we were planning for the coming years. We hadn't yet been to Italy, Prague, or Spain. There was so much more to explore together during this exciting opportunity. Birmingham, Alabama felt like an enormous slap in the face after the European dreams we'd built, but we PMA'ed our way through this international change of plans, two years into our marriage, in our mid-twenties.

We sat down together in our penthouse loft and made a list of what we could squeeze into the time we had in Europe. We went to Scotland, Ireland, and Wales, packing in two years' worth of new sites, foods and people into five days. We made the best of the time we had and would say "Positive Mental Attitude" frequently to each other.

Once back in the United States, we decided to eagerly look at Alabama as an unexpected twist in our story. Jay was pleasantly surprised with his professional assignment after a trip down to review the job and he convinced me it wasn't all trailers, stray dogs, and other stereotypical Alabama references. Together, we used PMA to set revised goals for a different chapter.

I explored job opportunities in Birmingham and found there was a new science museum looking for a development professional. We explored state parks and the running and biking scene in the area and found a surprising amount of activity. Jay even surprised me with a PMA diamond necklace as a sign of his gratitude for my flexibility and understanding as the U-Haul headed south from our home in Michigan.

Jay and I were an invincible team with our PMA. It wasn't that our life was perfect. We had our fair share of challenges. The difference, we thought, was that we were prepared, thoughtful, and optimistic. Our PMA tended to ensure that things worked out for us. And, they did.

Until one day we couldn't PMA our way out.

Cancer showed us, sometimes you need more than a Positive Mental Attitude. You need patience and grace and grit and love. When you face a challenge that can't be solved, only endured, you need HOPE. You need to cry and break and be vulnerable, because the hurt is deeper than positive thinking.

Our experiences facing cancer first while I was pregnant and then living with Stage 4 metastatic breast cancer for more than seven years made us realize positivity wasn't actually the key to a happy marriage. When the cancer mutated and became uncontrolled in spring of 2021, we were faced with bad news after bad news.

First, a surgery to help my lung was unsuccessful and I was left with a catheter to drain the fluid. Then, fluid started building up in my abdomen, which forced us to make the devastating shift to IV chemo. My strength, breath, and vibrancy started to fade. A scan following three months on the first chemo showed no improvement, so we moved to something stronger. A drain was added to my abdomen to drain fluid at home. I laid on the couch day after day, my legs propped up on pillows to lessen the swelling. Staring past my many plants in our big bay window, I watched the runners and walkers and moms pushing strollers go by, out living life. I felt disconnected from the world and myself, like I was in someone else's body. It was a body that was breathless, weak, and tired.

No amount of PMA could solve my problem. There was no way to fix it. We had to go deeper as a family. We could no longer hinge our joy, love and hope on things working out. We had to find a way to love and live regardless of what comes next.

I learned the "good vibes only" approach to life is impossible. Struggle is not something to triumph over or avoid, but rather, it is an inescapable part of life.

We all suffer. How we suffer matters.

PMA is the idea that if you stay positive, everything will be all right.

My concept of A Hopeful Life is allowing space for both suffering and joy, laughter and tears, winning and losing. Through this, we learn to live a deeper, more meaningful life. Having hope doesn't mean that my life is going to work out. Hope isn't contingent on the outcome.

I wish I could go back and tell those 22- and 25-year-old newlyweds in that Alaskan campground that the secret to life isn't PMA. It's hope.

Hope no matter what happens. When everything else is gone, hope is the understanding that we are made of love. We are made for love. We are made to love.

Life is not always positive. Things don't always work out.

And, yet, the bravest thing is, always hope.

MY HEART

BY LARA MACGREGOR

My heart

Place your hand on your heart. Feel its strong, steady beat.
This is you.
This is me.

Your heart grew from a few miraculous cells inside of me.
Creating you was the most amazing thing I ever did.

When I see your heart beat with dedication for something
you love - I see me in you.

When I see your heart beat for fairness and inclusion - I see
me in you.

When I see your heart beat strong and fast in competition - I
see me in you.

I will forever be a part of you. Put your hand on your heart.
Let the steady beat calm you and bring you back to the
essence of who you are.

This is you.

This is me.

MOM IS DYING

From the moment our babies are placed in our arms, moms have a mission to protect their precious charge. We are reborn as mothers, with a new purpose, perspective, and sense of love that has never been felt before. Being mom to Wills and Bennett is one of my greatest joys in this life, and I would do anything to keep them safe.

Yet, I will single-handedly be responsible for causing them the worst grief of their young lives by dying. This is one of the biggest fears I carry each day. I hope I will be the voice in their head that will help them and believe in them through their struggles, joys, and adventures.

All they know is cancer.

I was pregnant with Bennett and Wills was just two years old when I was first diagnosed with breast cancer. When I was diagnosed as metastatic in 2014, they were five and eight, and in kindergarten and 3rd grade. I remember pleading with God to give me five years.

On many sleepless nights, I knelt at their bedside and watched them sleep, my hand gently resting on their little backs, raising and lowering with their peaceful breath. With tears streaming down my face, I would pray to God to not break apart our family. Staring at their chubby, sleeping faces, I would find myself unable to breathe with the pain of leaving them.

Then, in the morning, I would hide in my bedroom until Jay got them ready for school because seeing them awake was too heartbreaking. I slowly gained my confidence to re-enter the world. I decided my goal would be to live long enough that they no longer called me "mommy" and were taller than me. These were benchmarks that would remind me how much they have grown and how much time we had together. Five years seemed like a lifetime when my mortality was crushing me daily.

This year, when we took our annual back to school photo as they started 11th and 8th grade, it occurred to me, "Here we are; we made it to my goal!" They are 13 and 16. Bennett passed me up in height this summer and I now have to look slightly up to see his bright blue eyes. Wills towers over both me and his dad at an astonishing 6'2" tall. Neither have called me mommy for years.

As I watched our two tall, kind, resilient boys walk to the car for their first day of school I sat down and cried. I was grateful to have made it to the goal I pleaded with God for all those years ago. But, I also realized how much more time I want to share together. I thought about all that we have endured since my diagnosis and how proud I was of our family for riding this MBC roller coaster together.

All they know is a mom with cancer, yet our life has been filled with more joy than tears. We've embraced life in ways others might take for granted. They saw me struggle but never give up, and they have watched how Jay takes care of me, and learned that we, Team Mac, are stronger together.

They are two teenage boys. It is a time in life when kids naturally pull away, stink, and prefer friends over parents, yet even now I am in awe of them. My love for them is as intense as the moment they were laid in my arms the first time.

In all honesty, I am also often frustrated, like any mom, with their "teenagerness." I grumble about the disgusting way they keep their room, the mood swings, the nine open cabinets in our kitchen. I may be facing a terminal illness, but they are still teenage boys. When I am exhausted on the couch from my toxic chemo, parenting doesn't stop. I still try to help edit English essays and ask them to sit with me for a moment before retreating to their bedrooms.

I engage with them on the experiences of their day, pulling out nuggets of information, as I remember how they used to blabber on and on about their fun days in preschool or elementary school. In these fleeting moments, I often hold their hand or place my hand on their arm.

They don't pull away. I love these moments of connection, even if the moments are fleeting. I just want to be with them.

I wish they wanted to be with me more, but I remind myself constantly of the age-appropriate nature of their choices. The fleeting time we have together makes me yearn for their love and connection.

As my body weakens from cancer progression and debilitating treatments, I am facing physical decline and emotional havoc. The hardest part is that as a result, I feel further from my children than ever before. I can't interact with them in the ways I always did - playing sports, doing projects together, driving them to activities, grabbing a smoothie, or taking big trips. So much of our life has been based on an active lifestyle. We go on family runs, we bike to breakfast, we hike together.

Now, they see me laying on the couch. They see their dad helping me to bed, draining fluid from my abdomen. They see me crying. Who we are as a family is lost just as much as who I am as a person has changed. Our home isn't filled with carefree laughter. We're not dashing off to fun activities or giddy with an impromptu kitchen dance party. It doesn't feel like us and I hate this for them. I feel our family slipping away even as we are all still right here together. Losing your life while you are living it is one of the hardest parts of facing a terminal illness.

Grief begins with denial and shock.

I used to get them up and out the door to school each morning, reminding them to grab the viola left in the dining room or the gym clothes folded on the counter. I was on top of all the mom details and loved it. Now, Jay manages the morning. If I am lucky, I pull myself out of bed long enough for a hug or they sneak in my room and give me a kiss before they leave. I wonder how hard it is to see other healthy moms living life with their families. I wonder if they miss the old me?

Our family is suffering. We each do it differently, but we are all in this together.

I know they love me. Our love is based on years of hugs, stories, snuggles and comfort. Parents of teenagers learn to live with less hugs and snuggles. But this is just bad timing. During this time in our family's story, I need to hold them close and find ways to connect. We must figure out how to do life right now; how to find connection and show up for each other, especially now. On a day I barely got out of bed after chemo treatment, I asked Jay if we could just have 30 minutes of family time together. What could that look like in this current reality? It had to look different than the many Funday Sundays of our past.

With Jay's creativity, it ended up being a picnic in our bed. The boys avoid my room and me in bed, but Jay made it approachable. They helped him make a big board of snacks and we set it up on a duffle bag in the middle of my bed. Everyone climbed in, limbs hanging off the edge. Two dogs tried to get in on the fun. We talked and laughed. I propped myself up on pillows and tried to choke down some of the charcuterie board.

We all remarked that it felt like Christmas morning. We have a tradition in our family that the kids get their stockings and bring them into our bedroom, and we all open the stockings in bed together. This simple moment together made my bed feel less like a sick, sad place. It brought love and laughter into a space that moments before hung with stagnant sadness.

Our picnic only lasted about 20 minutes, but it opened a new possibility. It became an open invitation for the boys to come into my room when I am sick in bed. The next day when I was resting in my room, I heard Bennett in the hallway after school. I asked him to come lay down with me and tell me about his day. He snuggled in and we talked for 30 minutes.

I said, "This is hard for me to face. I wonder if that's the same for you?"

I held his hand occasionally and stroked his bright red hair as he nodded. Later, when Wills got home from practice, I asked him to stop in and chat about his day. He was more reluctant, but I got a couple words and a quick hand hold. They have never seen their mom lay in bed. It's intimidating, but I am trying to show them, that inside this bony, bald body, it's still me. I must find ways to keep connecting with them. I am here now, even though it doesn't feel like us or me. We are still here, together.

When life was "normal" I talked with mom friends about parenting teenagers, home renovations, and cute dresses. It was all light, everyday stuff, not discussions of terminal cancer or a global pandemic. We talked about the idea that teenagers push us away, find their independence, define themselves, and eventually come back to us. We shared in the misery of how hard the pushing away is. We were comforted in the hope that we have given them skills and values to make good choices and guided by the anticipation that they come back around.

As I sit in the teenage world of my current reality, it hurts deeply that I won't get this "coming back." If I die in the middle of the teenage angst, we will miss all the connection and love that comes with maturity. I yearn so deeply to see them grow into the people they will become and to share my love with them in that phase and to feel their love back.

This is the beauty and curse of living well with a terminal illness - constantly modifying your dreams. At first, I just wanted them to be taller than me, but as I lived, and they grew, I saw them as teenagers and realized how amazing it would be to see them as young men. The possibility of staying in their lives seeps into your hope and changes as you have more time.

The time is a blessing, but it makes the acceptance that it is fleeting harder. There was a time, not too long ago, when my body was stable and healthy, that I allowed myself to see myself moving Wills into college. I saw myself walking Bennett out on the field for senior night. I even thought about actually being at one of their weddings. I allowed myself to dream, because I was strong and healthy and perhaps that would last longer than I had allowed myself to believe.

But then things changed, and the cancer went out of control. Now I am learning to accept that I will most likely not be here for the "coming back." I assure myself that Jay is very capable of moving Wills into college on his own and that Bennett will feel me on his arm, holding tightly, even if I am not physically there as he walks out as a senior onto that field.

I watch other tired, exhausted moms of teenagers complaining about their kids and the hoopla of college searches and all their activities, and I want to shake them and say, "You get to do this!" I wish they realized they are here - helping them pick a college, hounding them to finish their essays, asking them for the 10th time to not leave their stinky cleats in the middle of the living room, or begging them to bring their dishes back to the kitchen. It's not as snuggly and sweet as when they were little. Their sweet voices don't melt your heart with their spontaneous giggles. But, they are there. They get to watch them spread their wings, or struggle to find their way, or frustrate you with their bad decisions.

All I want is to be there.

As my heart breaks, I find comfort knowing that my love will be here. Always. I hope to teach our boys that they can send me their love, and that they will feel my love, just as if I was standing beside them, holding their hand.

If I'm not here for the coming back and the amazing things they will do in the future, then I will try to live as fully as possible in what we have right now. Eternity exists in the present.

I will be responsible for breaking their hearts, by dying, but I will also be the voice in their head that will help them go on. They will know how much I love them and believe in them.

Our love is what they will lean on to see them through. Always hope.

THE CIRCLE OF FRIENDSHIP

For about five years I lived in what I called the "time of stability, yet fear." My initial treatment for Stage 4 cancer was working, and I was learning to breathe again. I had to recreate my reality – I was no longer a breast cancer survivor who had faced cancer and put it behind her, but I also didn't feel like I was dying.

I was guided by a quote from one of my favorite authors, Kate Bowler. Her advice was inspiring to me during my time of stability. She writes in her book *Everything Happens for a Reason and Other Lies I've Loved*, "Think beyond cured and dying. Think, instead, about how to get from one good outcome to another."

This was a huge "a-ha" moment for me. I had been flailing between these two worlds. I couldn't put cancer behind me, but I was strong and capable. I didn't want to waste this time of stability on my fears of re-occurrence, yet I couldn't quite shake the impending doom. I started to see life in more variations – not just healthy or sick, strong, or weak - but a little bit of all of it at the same time.

In those initial days of diagnosis, treatments, and discussions about the future, not one doctor opened the door to the idea of living well with metastatic breast cancer. I understand they see patients progress rapidly, not respond to treatments, and decline on a regular basis. It would be cruel to offer false hope that this wouldn't also be my fate. I remember begging with a doctor to share any ideas of how I could live well with this new diagnosis.

I sat in his bland, sterile exam room, fresh off an all-night Google bender, determined to learn more about radical cancer remission. His knees occasionally bumping mine on that awkward swivel chair. I had a bruise between my eyes where a deep acupuncture needle had punctured a blood vessel. His first comment upon learning how I got the bruise was, "Trying it all, I see."

"Um, yeah," I chuckled back.

This was my life we were talking about. Despite the lack of hope he exuded, I knew he recognized my yearning. He just didn't have much to offer. He suggested a daily aspirin, and that felt like a cop out. If all he could suggest was aspirin, surely, I was doomed.

In the months that followed these initial diagnosis appointments, I realized that my inspiration wasn't going to come from medicine. I had to connect with patients, and I had to define what this was going to look like for me. I forced myself to stop watching radical videos about drinking my own urine or eating obscure mushrooms. I stopped ordering books and I stopped my deep dive internet sessions reviewing medical journals and clinical trial reports.

All of this made me more anxious. When faced with hard times in the past, I would connect with people. I'd go into nature, run, and breathe, and do yoga. I started doing more of this, letting go of what I felt I should do and more of what brought me comfort. I allowed myself to eat chips and guacamole and sip a cold beer with my husband. I was finally able to relax, just a little. Returning to myself was scary because what if a drastic change was indeed what would save me?

I nervously started asking myself "Is this life giving or life depleting?" I called this my joy filter, and I realized what brought me joy changed day to day. Some days a green smoothie chock full of spinach, spiranella, and ashwagandha brought me joy. Other days, it was truffle fries and an IPA.

I knew for certain it would be life-giving to find the stories of people living well with this disease. I signed up for support groups, Facebook groups, and conferences. Unfortunately, I didn't find what I was looking for right way with this approach either. The people on the support groups were hurting, struggling, and suffering. The Facebook group vibe was anger, with very little hope.

I attended the Living Beyond Breast Cancer conference for MBC in Philadelphia in the Spring of 2014. The conference, though scientifically informative, was incredibly overwhelming. I went to the conference seeking reassurance and hope, but instead, I felt the walls closing in around me. I went for a run most days, instead of sitting inside a hotel conference room falling deeper into despair.

As I felt my skin crawl, my heart break, and my butt numb on the uncomfortable chair in the far right corner of that beige conference room, I knew I had to get out of there. I slipped out the side door, went to my room, and changed into my running shoes. I walked out of the hotel and breathed a deep sigh of relief. I was back in the "normal" world where I was a healthy 38-year-old.

I ran up and down the river, the wind blowing in my hair, my legs strong, my heart pounding. After several miles I sprinted to a bench. I sat there, overlooking the flowing dark water, sweaty. While fixing my purple headband, my mind came back to the confused sense of dissolution of life I returned to repeatedly since my diagnosis. I was strong, healthy, and capable. I had Stage 4 cancer. I was dying. How are these things true?

When I finally walked back into the hotel, sweaty and in search of water, I went directly to the lobby Starbucks. There, I smiled at another young woman who had also apparently needed a break from the conference session. I said hello and introduced myself, realizing only afterwards that I must have seemed a little forward as I was no longer wearing the purple lanyard designating conference attendees as metastatic breast cancer patients.

I shared that I had MBC and asked what she thought of the conference. She shared that she too had MBC, but she looked confused. "Did you just go for a run?" she asked me with a chuckle.

I smiled, "Yes, I had to get some fresh air and clear my head."

She clarified again that I had MBC. I answered, "Yes. In my sacrum."

"Impressive," she responded. We laughed together and started up a conversation about our diagnosis and discovered we both found a lump in the shower while pregnant. We talked about our kids, treatments, hopes, and worries.

Connecting with Gina confirmed my hunch, that there were people living well with this disease. Those people were living, not spending Tuesday night on a support group call, or ranting on Facebook.

They were traveling, taking their kids to practices, working, dreaming, and living!

My roommate at the conference, Meghan, was the first person I reached out to when I was diagnosed with MBC. I met Meghan at a Young Survival Conference in New Orleans years before, when I was still basking in the "glory" of early-stage survivorship and launching Hope Scarves. She was diagnosed metastatic from the start in 2011, at just 29 years old. When she stopped by our Hope Scarves exhibit booth, I was instantly drawn to her bright light and smile. We were just putting this big dream of Hope Scarves out into the world, and I was eager to talk with people about my ideas.

Meghan asked good questions, her blue-green eyes showing her authentic interest in the answers, not just free swag. She tapped the brochure in her hand and said, "Do you want metastatic stories?"

I must admit, in my pre-MBC naiveté, I hadn't much considered this. In my happy world of cancer survivorship, Hope Scarves was sharing inspirational stories of overcoming cancer. I wasn't quite sure what to do with a story from someone who hadn't "beat" cancer, yet, here I was, eye-to-eye with this beautiful red-headed young woman clearly filled with strength, wellness, and hope.

My immediate emotion was sorrow for her. How terrible it was to be MBC from the start – to never be given the chance to put cancer behind you. I was in awe of her easy smile, despite this death sentence. From this quick interaction, a friendship blossomed, she shared her story with Hope Scarves, and allowed us to use her beautiful pictures on our website. She helped me see the importance of sharing all stages of cancer, and when I was faced with the unthinkable recurrence of cancer, she eased my fears with her gentle kindness.

As I grappled with the MBC diagnosis, I asked Meghan if she knew anyone else living well with MBC and if we could start a text group. I didn't envision an official support group, but instead, I wanted a group of women who were living and loving life despite an MBC diagnosis. We soon created "Friends over MBC" which was a text string that lasted for years.

I needed to rely on them that I would find reassurance in this deadly world. I discussed being at a girls' beach trip and feeling like I couldn't connect with my friends. There we were, sitting in the brilliant sunshine, longtime friends facing each other in a circle of beach chairs in the powdery sand, passing magazines, sunscreen, and bottles of wine around. It was an annual trip I looked forward to each year as a chance to catch up on each other's families, pop culture, summer salad recipes, and book recommendations.

Days were filled with easy conversations among friends, our talks peppered with spontaneous laughter moving easily from problem-solving teenage dramas or kitchen remodeling projects, decisions about careers, and travel dreams. We also found solace in heavier topics like raising a special needs child, helping aging parents, and tough conversations with spouses.

But that year, as we talked, I found I was grateful for our friendship but felt like none of them could understand how different life was when all this was happening in the context of a terminal illness. I knew they loved me and supported me, but my fears, worries, and dreams were just so different from theirs as I faced my mortality.

When all my friends were getting ready to go out to a fun dinner, I snuck away in tears and texted our MBC group asking for help. My friend Brandi texted me right back and shared a similar experience, and reassured me that it was normal to feel this way. One woman in the group, Katherine, was our group's mama hen. She had faced MBC for over 15 years and lived through so many of the roller coasters of emotions we all were feeling. Her steadfast reassurance grounded us.

One day at a time. One day at a time.

Our MBC group shared kid's achievements, physical accomplishments, and trips. We shared support to Meghan, who bravely watched all of us raising families, but was never able to have children of her own. We celebrated each other's perseverance. They were what I was looking for – strong, beautiful women beating the odds, and living life over cancer:

Colleen	Wendie
Roberta	Katherine
Marcia	Brandi
Shayne	Meghan

We were fierce! Until we weren't. One by one our group began to falter. A scan showed progression. A new lesion in the brain appeared. We endured toxic treatments with debilitating side effects.

I watched as this group of women who were vibrant, free, and determined, died. They tried to cling to their early lives, cherishing simple moments, sharing snapshots that made them smile that day, but, one by one they left this earth. They left behind families who would never be whole again. Over the course of a couple of years the text string went from eight to four, and then, to just Meghan and me.

This group was powerful for me, as an example of women living life over MBC. I needed them to help rebuild my life and help me believe that I too could live a full, beautiful life. What did I learn in their tragic deaths? I learned that the living and dying is all wrapped into one. These brave women helped each of us walk into death together. They showed me how to live, and they showed me how to die.

Today, cancer is progressing in my body, and I face many unknowns. My body is weaker than it has ever been in my lifetime. Meghan, by the way, is hiking in Michigan's Porcupine Mountains as I write this. She is strong, and well, and free. Thank God for Meghan, who was always my example of health and joy. She was a little ahead of me on this journey, and I looked to her example to see how my life might unfold.

I'm grateful I gave myself the chance to be open to the possibility of wellness and joy and laughter way back at the start of this. Instead of fearing the inevitable and waiting for the cancer to progress, I lived! I embraced my wellness with radical hope, and the result is that in those five years of stability yet fear I wasn't chained to my fears.

I was guided by my hope.

LETTING HOPE SCARVES GO

Today, as my health falters, I am in the process of handing over Hope Scarves leadership to our first executive director. I always planned to step away from the day-to-day operations of Hope Scarves. I've read enough leadership books to recognize the significance of the founder stepping aside to let the organization run on its own. I knew this day would come, but I didn't expect it to be under these circumstances. I am not healthy enough to lead Hope Scarves in the way I always have and the way it needs to be led. I leave weak and broken, but the organization is thriving.

When I imagined handing off leadership to Hope Scarves it was planned to be for the pursuit of my next big idea, My Hopeful Life. My dream for My Hopeful Life, which was launched in January 2020, was for it to be an extension of Hope Scarves, where I would dig more deeply into my own story and what it means to live a Hopeful Life. It would include a film, blog, speaking engagements, podcast, and this book.

It is anchored in the website, www.myhopefullife.org. It extends beyond cancer to anyone facing hard times with the idea of finding joy, not because the issue is solved or the crisis past, but in how you live through the struggle. As I planned out the project, it became the thing that was life-giving to me.

At a small gathering in January in my friend's interior design industrial loft space, I shared my vision and samples of storytelling to launch My Hopeful Life. I had been sharing my story through Hope Scarves for years, eagerly hopping on stage after stage to promote my dream and the work of our organization. It happened naturally (and successfully) year after year.

For some reason, telling my story and going out on my own was totally different, and terrifying. The evening of the launch event, as the studio filled with eager people, I locked myself in the bathroom. My heart was racing, my hands shook as I tried to put on lipstick. I held onto both sides of the white porcelain sink, staring at myself in the mirror. Who did I think I was? Why do I think I can create a project based around my story? This whole project is so self-righteous. Why did I leave the safety and love of the Hope Scarves mission? This was a terrible idea.

Deep breaths. Deep breaths. A knock on the door, "Are you OK, Lara?" kindly came from the other side.

I opened the door slightly, and said, "Yup. Just going to need a couple minutes."

With a reassuring smile, a glass of champagne was handed to me.

"You can do this," said my friend.

These four words were the same message Kelley had written on the box of scarves she mailed to me 14 years earlier.

Minutes later, in a brilliant, flowered dress, I nervously walked out and presented four stories that would represent the concept of My Hopeful Life. I had a videographer there to capture my public speaking for promotion and the website.

I flopped. Now, my friends and husband may disagree, but I basically presented what I think is the worst public speaking engagement of my life. When I watch the film, I want to puke, all over again. I am so nervous, and I can't relax, and I keep fidgeting with my notes. It is uncomfortable to watch, let alone use as a speaking sample.

A friend later told me, "You did great, but I have never seen you nervous before." That half compliment clearly reinforced my notion. It sucked.

While I may never use the speaking samples, but the event served as a deadline for me to "jump" into my dream. It created a public space for me to say, I was pursuing a new dream. It allowed me to start to understand that I was worthy. I was not a fraud or imposter. My story and this idea for My Hopeful Life had merit.

On March 8, 2020, we hosted an all-day strategic planning retreat with our staff and board to dream about the future. My Hopeful Life emerged as one of the key focus areas. I was stepping into my new dream. We talked about staff structure, integration, and communication strategies. I was excited for this new chapter for both me and Hope Scarves. With the help of our board and our strategic planning consultants, I could see that the best way for me to serve Hope Scarves was no longer leading staff meetings or planning fundraising events. My story had far more potential.

Days later, we closed our doors as the world faced a global pandemic.

Immediately, I started figuring out what this meant for Hope Scarves. We closed for two weeks as our staff got their bearings with kids learning virtually, safety concerns, and heightened anxiety. Coming together on Zoom, we created a plan. Our staff would come in on a rolling basis, so no one was in the office together. We fulfilled Hope Scarves requests by masking and gloving up to be safe. We left each shipment in "quarantine" for a week before putting it in the mail as advised by a local doctor.

Through the pandemic, we never stopped supporting people facing cancer. Instead, our numbers steadily rose. We realized that as hospital resource centers closed and people had more time online, an increasing number of people found us. And, they needed us. Facing cancer in the midst of a pandemic was terrifying.

Days earlier, I was stepping away from Hope Scarves. Now, I was entrenched in our mission and survival, without a second thought. I re-imaged fundraisers, created the "Hope Isn't Canceled" campaign celebrating women facing cancer through the pandemic, and we launched a recurring giving program. I researched the PPP loan and worked with our finance coordinator to secure this support. I led the board and staff through follow-up sessions of our strategic planning process that seemed a bit futile in such an uncertain time.

I was proud to work side-by-side with our staff and see the important role Hope Scarves played as a support, community, and resource to cancer patients through the pandemic.

Despite my intentional focus on leading Hope Scarves, I tried not to lose sight of my dreams for My Hopeful Life. I created a series of Instagram videos I called "From Cancer to COVID," connecting the experience of facing cancer to what many were feeling during the pandemic. There was one on not living in the perceived future, one on doing it afraid, and another encouraging people to ground yourself in gratitude.

Every time I hit the record button, I felt a bit like an imposter, but I had to be true to my dream. As kind comments and support followed, I realized my messages were comforting and impactful. I kept telling myself, you can do this.

Weeks turned into months, then years of the pandemic, and my role was clear, ensuring the sustainability of Hope Scarves. I created successful virtual fundraisers, reimagined events for 500 guests, and when our yearly marathon fundraiser was canceled, I created an international Outrunning Cancer experience with participants around the globe. Hope Scarves thrived with creativity, grit and grace. Our team was amazing. I helped the organization pivot, again and again, as we found our way.

As the pandemic raged, I experienced the first bad cancer news in years. Fluid was again crushing my lung. I changed treatments and tried to balance the mounting anxiety and fear of cancer and COVID. People talk about losing a year during the bizarre reality of the pandemic. People lost loved ones, businesses, and careers. Important events like marriages, funerals, and graduations were canceled. It was a terrible time for millions. Life changed for everyone in some way.

There wasn't a moment when I decided to officially step away from leadership of Hope Scarves. It was more a series of small moments that helped me see it was time. I was going to do it my way when I launched My Hopeful Life and I was healthy and the world was normal. Then, I didn't, because Hope Scarves needed me throughout the pandemic. I needed the purpose and creative outlet to guide the organization. It was a great distraction in the early months of progression. As the cancer got worse, there were a series of moments when I realized I was no longer the leader I always was. I was no longer the leader that Hope Scarves needed.

While the idea of stepping away from Hope Scarves in these

circumstances is agonizing, I am grounded in gratitude that it has become something bigger than me. My story will always be part of the founding and my vision guiding the work of staff and volunteers will last for decades to come. I raised this little idea into a dynamic, successful, important organization. The fact that it isn't going to die when I do brings me immense joy. It is my legacy.

My Hopeful Life is also still moving forward. Despite the pandemic, I launched a podcast, recording 20 episodes in what might be both the first and last season. I shared beautiful conversations with people facing a range of heartbreak, from losing a spouse, paralyzing accidents, gun violence and more. The podcast conversations are both tragic and beautiful, just like the lives of the storytellers.

And, if you are reading this in a real-life book, I published the book! Hopefully, I will live long enough to see it myself, hold it in my hands, and maybe even connect with readers to discuss how it resonates with them.

If I don't, please take a deep breath. Do me a forever favor. Hold this book to your chest and go live your own Hopeful Life.

CHOOSE JOY

BY LARA MACGREGOR

Savor each day.
Jump in. Get your hair wet.
Let a sunset take your breath away.
Hold both joy and fear in the same hand, at the same time.
Choose joy, not because everything is OK, but because you
believe in hope and love in the midst of the struggle.

Don't look for the light at the end of the tunnel.

Be the light - right here, where you are.

With love,

Lara

A FAREWELL

As 2021 progressed, Lara's health declined. She lived and loved her dream of appearing on ABC's "Good Morning America" in October. On a brisk, sunny morning, family and friends joined Lara for mimosas and cheers, as she watched her story unfold to a nationwide audience. The joy in her eyes was mesmerizing to all who watched alongside her.

She nurtured a secret that day as well, that only a few in attendance shared. In just a few weeks' time, Lara was named an international "Woman of Worth" by cosmetics giant L'Oreal Paris. The award highlights the philanthropic achievements of ten leaders nationwide who are making meaningful progress in addressing society's most pressing issues.

She was desperate to make the trip to Paris, France for the celebrations, but her health would not allow that. Instead, L'Oreal came to Kentucky and a film crew helped Lara tell her story and celebrate this cherished international honor. When L'Oreal announced the awards, Lara enjoyed widespread media coverage and accolades, and was able to participate in a nationally broadcast hour-long special, "Women of Worth", which aired on ABC television just before Christmas 2021.

Lara shared the holidays with family close by, but as the year came to a close, she knew her time was limited. Cancer consumed her frail body, but her spirit remained strong. She fought with every breath to live as long and as strong as she could.

Lara Plewka MacGregor found peace and endless sailing on her beloved waters on January 18, 2022. She was just 45 years old. Although Lara's time on earth was short, her memory and legacy lives on within us. She taught us how to hold joy and fear in the same hand at the same time, to live a great story, and to always hope.

She was a resilient, brave, and loving soul who inspired thousands with her message of living a hopeful life. Since its founding in 2012, Hope Scarves has sent over 30,000 scarves to every state and 34 countries to people facing over 90 different types of cancer. With the news of Lara's metastatic diagnosis in 2014, Hope Scarves has also raised one million dollars to further metastatic breast cancer research.

But, in addition to creating connections across the globe through Hope Scarves and A Hopeful Life, more than anything, Lara loved creating memories with Team Mac - her husband and two boys. She loved to spend time cheering on her boys at sports games, reading and writing at her family farm, and spending time outdoors. Each summer, she enjoyed living life to the fullest with family and friends by her side in the great Lake Michigan waters - her home and happy place. Lara never took a second for granted and was always willing to jump in and get her hair wet.

As the new year dawned, Lara recorded the following message for friends and family. We share parts of it here, as a farewell from Lara.

She will be missed and treasured by all her family and friends forever. As she would say, live out loud.

Live every day. And always hope.

Hello, my lovelies.

When I was originally diagnosed with breast cancer 14 years ago, I endured all the care, the double mastectomy, reconstruction, and was deemed cancer free for about seven years. And it was amazing. I lived such a great life, recognizing how precious and fragile it is. Having been diagnosed at age 30 while I was pregnant, it definitely put a new perspective on our life, and I feel like we just lived so fully in those years, raising our kids and taking advantage of everything that was available to us.

In 2014, I was diagnosed with metastatic breast cancer – a disease that has an average life expectancy of two-to-three years and kills 114 people every day. I lived with metastatic disease for eight years and lived the best way I knew how. We sought out the best doctors, and I set myself on a wellness path that would allow me to live even in the uncertainty of metastatic disease.

I've lived so fully. I ran half marathons, I climbed mountains, I slept in rainforests, I cheered our children on in games, I climbed sand dunes and we surfed and just lived a full, full life in those eight years. No one would've guessed that I was as sick as I was.

I think a lot of people were confused during this time of health for me, but I was an exceptional responder. My treatments were working, and I lived so fully. (When the cancer returned) I started IV chemo this summer and I did pretty well on it. I was still able to have such a great summer, and swim, and sail, and surf, and be with my children. I didn't feel 100%, but I wasn't going to let cancer steal that summer… and we didn't.

Unfortunately, when we came back from Michigan, we found out that the chemo I was on wasn't really doing a good enough job, so we switched to a harder chemo called Trodelvi and that's what I've been on since August. At the same time, I've just seen my body get weaker and weaker, and it's been frustrating, because while the cancer appears to not be out of control, my body is out of control in its decline.

After an ambitious fall family trip out west to the Grand Canyon and Zion National Park, we celebrated my birthday in Boca Raton, Florida with my family. We traveled to New York to receive the L'Oreal Paris 2021 Women of Worth award.

We have decided to enter Hospice care. We are prioritizing being home with our family, instead of racing around to hospitals and doctors' appointments and chemo treatments. My counselor explained to me that as you get closer to death, your circle becomes smaller and smaller.

It's so true. You start with this big giant circle, and it includes all your friends, your kids' friends, moms from school, and the ladies in your running club, and the entire class, and your book club, and all these different people. And then, as you get closer and closer, it just becomes quieter.

And that's where we are right now, just recognizing the joy and the specialness, being quiet and together, and helping me find some pain management and some sleep. We're addressing all that together with the Hospice nurses. I'm in very good hands.

I appreciate you allowing me to have this time to be reflective and be with my family, and I'm so grateful for this community of people who care about us, and love us, and want to see us find a miracle. I enter Hospice still hopeful, very, very, very hopeful.

Feel free to send up prayers for peace and understanding. Pray for our children who are processing all this in the midst of being teenage boys, and that's a lot. Pray for Jay to be able to balance his work commitments with his caregiving commitments, because he's doing an amazing job.

It's been an amazing ride, but I would've turned back these 14 years in a heartbeat, and given it all away to live a mediocre, normal life. But instead, this is where we are, and I wouldn't change anything.

I have no regrets. I'm so grateful for the people I've met, the experiences I've had, the lessons I've learned, and the opportunities that I've had.

It's been incredible. Thank you.

Go enjoy your day. This morning I was thinking how special it was, when I heard the garbage truck running by, and I thought, "Oh, I'll just swing my leg over the bed and run out there and get the garbage out in time." Even that is a gift to be able to do, so don't take it for granted.

My wish for you is every day, live it up, love deeply, and tell people you love them.

Go love your people. Celebrate your one precious light.

Always hope.

Lara

LARA MACGREGOR
1976-2022

OUR HOPEFUL LIVES

Our Hopeful Lives
captures the experiences of people
across the country who faced devastating
challenges and found a way to thrive - not because
the threat was resolved or they found the light at the
end of the tunnel. They understand that struggle is part
of the story. It is not something to run away from or fix, but
instead, messily live with to find peace. Each of these stories are
unique. No two face the same hardship, yet the singular question,
our "golden thread" winds its way through each story. "How can I
live a Hopeful Life, regardless of what comes next?"

This section shines a spotlight on their beautiful stories. This section
is deeply personal for them. But, I know the power of the ripple
and once these stories get out there, there will be hundreds, if not
thousands, who relate or find perspective in their life because of the
bravery of these powerful storytellers.

My sincere thanks to these contributors, who shared their stories
with author Laura Ross, for so bravely showing their vulnerability
so all the world can see how they shine.

NEVER GIVE UP

TOM MORRIS

Life can change in an instant. Tom Morris knows that all too well.

Tom Morris always aimed high. A stellar athlete, he loved sports and set his sights on a career in coaching. He began his career in the athletic departments at Pennsylvania's La Salle University and later at Pennsylvania State University, before taking a coveted job at Indiana University as a strength and conditioning coach.

During this busy time, he married his sweetheart, Christa, and spent hours training for and running many races, triathlons, and even a half-Ironman race in 2010. His goal was to prepare for the grueling Ironman competition, which is one of the greatest tests of endurance an elite athlete can face.

Little did he know that soon, he would face his ultimate challenge.

May 17, 2012, started out like any other day for Tom. He arrived to work at Indiana University at 6 a.m. to train the women's basketball program and a handful of the men's soccer team. By 8:30 a.m., he was finished and looking forward to a trail ride on his bike through the Indiana trails he loved. He was training for a race that weekend and had already conquered some of the toughest bike and trail races in the country. He felt on top of the world physically and mentally.

"Everything was great, but on the fourth lap of the ride, I came around a turn, flipped over the handlebars, rotated through the air and came down on my head," he said. Tom instantly shattered his C6 and C7 vertebrae.

He landed in the woods, where he would lay for three long hours.

"I couldn't move. It was not only my legs, but I couldn't feel my upper body. My hands did not work at all, and it must have been 15 minutes into this when I finally got my bearings," he explained.

While he knew he had suffered a catastrophic injury, he didn't let fear consume him. "It was strange and weirdly peaceful," he said. Tom focused on the heart and breathing monitors on his watch and fought to maintain stability in his breathing and heart rate. He felt as if he was "suction-cupped to the ground."

There was no way to find help. He couldn't reach his phone. He couldn't move. He was completely alone in the woods.

The first hour, he fought to move. The second hour, the pain seared through his body with a fire he'd never known. The third hour felt like an evil reckoning. His breath was shallow, and his heart rate was dropping. He feared he would never survive.

Eventually, two riders came by, and Tom was transported to hospitals in Bloomington and later, Indianapolis, where he underwent surgery and initial rehabilitation.

This super athlete, young, strong man, and active coach faced a future with a broken neck that resulted in paralysis below his shoulders.

Life had changed in an instant.

Always the optimist and consummate fighter, Tom initially fought the realization that he was severely injured. All the powerful thinking in the world though, slammed into a brutal reality on the fifth day following his accident.

He started rehabilitation and said that he realized walking again was the least of his worries. He had lost all independence and for Tom, that was a "sobering and humbling feeling."

"It wrecked my world," he said. "On that fifth day, I had to make a choice of how I was going to continue to evolve and continue to keep living. I cried with my wife's head on my chest, and I was laying there, not knowing where to turn. But I made the decision at that point, that when I woke up on the sixth day, that that's how I was going to live. I was going to do everything I could and not sit there and dwell on what happened."

That mindset catapulted Tom towards his new reality. "I thought of this quote by the author of the Harry Potter novels, JK Rowling, because I had heard it so many times, but it never resonated with me until that moment. Rowling wrote, 'Rock bottom became the solid foundation on which I rebuilt my life.'"

He systematically began to claw up from rock bottom.

"I had to control what I could control," Tom explained. He fought through the stages of grief and knew he had to win the battle past anger and denial and move towards an actionable plan.

"I believe that once you accept what happened, you're able to gain your strength, your power, and your ability to live and keep moving forward. I got up every single day and just tried to work on the littlest of things," he said.

Tom would get frustrated in rehab that he couldn't pinch his finger, yet he realized that he *could* pinch his finger. "Every day was closer. I got my pointer finger to my thumb. And then, the middle finger to the thumb was harder. But soon, I could move all five fingers right down my hand. I could control that."

"I couldn't focus then on the future goal of walking," he added. "Every day, I worked on the little things, knowing that it would lead to the big picture later."

He fought through his initial rehabilitation and later, was transferred to Frazier Rehab Institute in Louisville, Kentucky for intensive therapy.

Tom was able to regain arm movement and a significant amount of hand function through physical and occupational therapies. As an outpatient at Frazier Rehab, he participated in the NeuroRecovery Network program. His rehabilitation included the groundbreaking locomotor training, researched and pioneered in part through the University of Louisville's Dr. Susan Harkema.

Locomotor training helps the spinal cord remember how to walk.

In the NeuroRecovery Network program, locomotor training is an activity-based therapy treadmill training. Three therapists assisted Tom in a harness that was attached to a hydraulic treadmill that supported a portion of his body weight. The therapists worked to pattern a normal gait with him.

As a professional athletic trainer, Tom was accustomed to encouraging others to work hard and achieve their goals. Doctors and therapists watched Morris inspire patients his own age, as well as elderly and pediatric patients.

"A year later, I came out of rehab, came back to my job at IU, and started training athletes again," he explained.

"This is not a death sentence," Tom added. "I have great health. I have great energy and I'm just continuing. The minute I start feeling bad for myself, I think I've been blessed with the gift of breath every day, so why not take advantage of that? I have a great job, family, and community. I don't dwell on the wheelchair. You must enjoy life every day, no matter what your situation is. You have the gift of breath each day. Use it."

When he returned to his coaching position at IU, Tom called it the best rehab he could face. "The biggest thing I realized was that people didn't see me in a wheelchair. I told the athletes I didn't want the chair to inspire them. I wanted to inspire them."

He was once again with the athletes he loved and found his peace and motivation. He now is the Senior Assistant Athletic Director for Athletic/Sports Performance at Indiana University. He continues to strength train and coach the athletes with a passion and story that is uniquely his own. Many times, the athletes motivate Tom to pursue his own strength conditioning – both physically and mentally.

"Two months after returning to my job at IU, I got on a hand cycle for the first time and it brought back all the stuff that I've always done before," he said. He quickly moved up the ranks in the world of hand cycling and began racing at the national level.

It wasn't an easy ride, though, by any stretch.

Coaching was Tom's dream, but as much as he loved motivating his student athletes, he knew his toughest critic was himself. He knew the impact and influence he could bring, despite his disability. "I wanted to get back to a life where I lived independently. As a coach – and a person – I could still impact people, push them physically, mentor them, and create joy. I say I'm a realistic optimist," he laughed.

A realistic optimist, Tom said, is someone who realizes some things are out of your control, but you push forward with enthusiasm. There's no guarantee of success, but you can work on what works for you, and control those elements. Each day is a win on some level. Tom made a point of waking up each day, looking in a mirror, and stating a positive intention.

"It gave me an incredible amount of strength and an ability to keep moving forward," he said. "And when things got tough, I kept saying it out loud and kept moving in a direction that allowed me momentum to improve the smallest things. Those small things underlie the fact that I am alive today. And it's a really great life in so many ways."

A career in athletics was destiny for Tom, and the synonymous trajectories of training and rehabilitation are key to his success today. "Athletics is such a microculture of what the real world is like," he explained. "If you want to win a national championship, you've got to win your first game. But to win your first game, you've got to prepare. You must get up the right way in the morning, you need to eat the right food, put your shoes on the right way, get to practice, and get to work. Those are the little things that make the big things possible."

"Athletics teach us to take care of the little things, so you can reach that big goal," he added. "But it also shows you, sometimes brutally, that you can do everything right, and still not grab that title. Sometimes, the ball or the call just doesn't go your way. For me, that was important to realize personally, because I understood I didn't have to have the end result of walking again. I would love to walk again, but I don't need that ability to be a whole person. I am happy in the present moment – and that's all I've got. And it's good."

"We are not guaranteed the next minute, hour, or even second in front of us," Tom said. "Not worrying constantly about what's in front of you and what you can and can't do is one of the most undervalued skills you can have. It's so incredibly powerful to live in the moment, no matter what adversity you face. You win each moment."

For many, it takes a village. Tom surrounded himself with family, friends, coworkers, student athletes, and medical professionals who helped him face each challenge. From the early days of his injury to the present, he learned to rely on help he needed, when he needed it.

"I was completely dependent on others at the beginning," Tom explained. "I needed help with everything from going to the bathroom to having others push me around, because my body atrophied, and the neuro-connectivity was nil. I worked for years to get to this point now where I've regained strength in my upper body and am much more independent. I can drive now, I work, I'm involved in sports again, and I'm the husband I was before the accident."

Tom's wife Christa has been by his side continually and is his rock. "Christa is the coach of my team," Tom laughed. "She knows me better than anyone. She was the first person at the hospital that day, and she is my organizer, my coach, my cheerleader, my trainer, so many things. She is so freaking strong that I just feel like I can do anything when she's by my side."

Tom noted that it's often equally as hard for the closest around you to watch a loved one struggle. "I know it's been hard for her to watch me come forward from this injury," he said. "I think being on the outside looking in is a really big challenge, but the way she's handled it and what she's done for me, and so many others, is so incredible because she's just so strong and so awesome."

Team Morris works daily to gain new wins for Tom. In addition to his wife and family, friends, and sometimes, even strangers, lift him up. "It's been huge energy," he explained. "I just love the fact that they were so there for me, sometimes traveling hours to see me. When you have people that are there to care and love on you with this positive, optimistic energy, you feel like you have this almost super-human strength. It was the reason I got up every day. I wanted to make sure I was living up to their wishes for me. They made the effort for me, and it was my responsibility to make the effort to get well for them."

While the critical days of his traumatic injury have passed, Tom still is moved by encounters he has with others today. He knows the kindness of his close friends and supporters, but sometimes a chance meeting gives him a needed boost. A simple trip to the DMV introduced Tom to a clerk who recognized his name and knew his story instantly, years later. She was the original dispatcher who covered the ambulance run on his accident in 2012. She told Tom that even though they didn't know each other, everyone in the dispatcher's office that day started praying for him.

"As that guy laying in the woods, I felt that," Tom said. "It was just an energy, and I felt I could not fail. Those people made up my team, whether they knew it or not, and they continue to help me all these years later. It's so important to have that support, whether it's through prayer, good thoughts, or a literal hand to lift you. Support comes from so many levels."

Tom encourages everyone, even if it's uncomfortable, to share that support. Say "I'm thinking of you," or ask if there's anything a person needs that day, he explained. It could be a ride to a doctor's appointment, or it could be as easy as telling a joke to pull up a smile. Those moments often mean more for the person struggling than any bigger gesture.

In addition to his busy coaching career at IU, Tom took his story on the road and is currently a motivational speaker for many events and organizations. He hopes he can motivate others as much as he does his athletes, but without, perhaps, lifting as many weights or running as many laps, he laughed. "My journey is continually moving forward, but it's given me a perspective on life, about growth, and about doing things that are hard. No matter what, you just keep doing the hard stuff, because it's going to make the future, and the reward, so much better."

In communicating his story to others, he hopes to make a positive influence where hope might be lost. "It's truly remarkable how it makes you feel," he said. 'When I'm helping someone, I'm not paying attention to my own bad days. If I can have a conversation with someone who is in a tough situation, who might not have that team supporting them, it uplifts me."

Not everyone wants to hear a cheery, "You can do it!" sometimes, Tom admitted. "I remember visiting a young man in the hospital with a gunshot wound. He was completely alone, with no support. To him, that was it. Life over. He was in a bad place. Our entire conversation for a week straight was about Louisville football, which I don't follow at all, but of course, I love football. It was our common theme, and as we bantered back and forth, we found common ground. I told him he had a future. And, where days earlier, he wasn't in that space, this time, he listened."

Many times, you just need to listen. "My story isn't your story," Tom added. "I am an example of how to live in positive way, after a terrible accident, but the motivation comes in listening and thinking through how your experience could help someone facing their own mountain. It's not just sitting there and saying, hey, listen man, keep your head up, everything's going to be all right. I think just showing empathy of being there sometimes and listening to someone talk about life is what is meaningful. I don't have all the answers, but I can listen to your fears and thoughts and help you work through those moments."

"I hate when someone says, 'I know what you mean,'" Tom added. "No, you don't. You don't have a clue about my deep story. No one does. It doesn't matter if you're paralyzed, have cancer, or your spouse left you. Each one of us has such a unique story and it's our perspectives that all come together in a certain way to help each other. The only way we heal is to listen to each other, find common ground, and learn how to move forward."

The daily fight reminds Tom of those other elite warriors, the Navy SEALS, who have their lives on the line frequently as they face adversity most will never know. "The Navy SEALS have the ability, even in the heat of battle, to pause and step back," Tom said. "It's about gaining a different perspective, often quickly, to make the right leadership decision. Personally, I see the worth in changing your perspective, even when it's difficult or frightening.

There are times when you need your team. You need to pause, and say, hey, I need help. We all have those moments when you must admit, it sucks right now. But it's imperative to have the gratitude and fortitude to put life on pause and step into a unique perspective.

I think it's so important to lean on your team to find the good things you have and put into words the acceptance of things you can't control. You must acknowledge this is your life, now, today, and probably tomorrow. Do what you can to make it the best it can be."

As 2020 dawned and the pandemic roared into the world, Tom adjusted his sails again. He was deeply involved in coaching at IU and building the momentum and energy of the entire athletic department, which was reaching new heights each day and season. His speaking career was also taking off and he was living his passion of delivering hope and inspiration to others. And then, the world shut down.

Like most things in his life, he pivoted. He took up podcasting appearances and spoke regularly on Zoom meetings. His story didn't fall into the cracks of COVID-19. He followed his own advice to live for the moment.

Even on hard days, Tom remains motivated.

"I never judge myself on the hard days," he said. "If I'm down and don't feel well, maybe I have 15% to give that day. I used to get really frustrated with myself, and worry about the big picture, but I've found the less I judge myself, the kinder I am to myself. If I've only got 15% right now, if that's all I have for an entire day? I'm going to give it and give it until I can't, and I'll just chalk it up to today. Tomorrow will be better.

And if tomorrow I wake up and it's like this, I'll address it tomorrow. We can't think about the future and all these things that potentially could happen, but more than likely aren't going to happen. Living that moment instead didn't just bounce me out of the hole, it let me be kinder to myself and not make that hole so deep to start.

Once you build that energy and inspire people around you, there's momentum that's shifted because at the end of the day, life is all a momentum game. It's about the tiny little things in life that add up to creating momentum to keep moving forward. And even when adversity strikes, it's being able to take that derailment of momentum and then get it back online and move forward.

That is what creates positive growth and joy. And, of course, hope."

EZRA SPEAKS

THE FREAUF FAMILY

"It's about saying their names as much as possible. We are giving these babies purpose, and their lives are changing other people's lives, even if that is simply providing support for their loss," said Lauren Freauf, quietly, but firmly.

She knows. Deeply and profoundly. Love can be wrapped in heartbreak but warmed with hope.

Lauren Freauf and her husband Ross had fresh dreams for their futures. The young couple met shortly after Lauren, a native of Louisville, Kentucky, took a leap and moved to Dallas, Texas in 2011. Lauren and Ross met at a Christmas party, built their relationship, and were married in April 2016. They were thrilled to welcome their first son, Wells, in May 2018. Life was good – careers were blossoming, friends were plentiful, and their vivacious little boy with a shock of platinum curls delighted everyone who met him.

Good news arrived again for the Freauf family in the tumultuous spring of 2020 when Lauren learned she was pregnant again. "My first thought was people were going to say, 'Oh, a pandemic baby!' and I really didn't want that to be a part of my child's story, since we'd been trying to get pregnant long before the pandemic arrived," laughed Lauren. "I should've known God had a bigger plan."

Ross and Lauren told their families the good news over Easter Zoom visits, due to the pandemic keeping everyone quarantined. Despite the world of COVID-19, Lauren's pregnancy progressed naturally, until an unexpected phone call arrived in June.

Routine bloodwork – that sadly, did not have a routine result – prompted a call to Lauren from her OBGYN. "I was alone and sitting in my car and the doctor's office called," she explained. "My doctor said the bloodwork came back with flags for Trisomy 18. I had no idea what that meant, but I thought, OK, a child with potential special needs. We can handle that."

What Lauren didn't expect were words that followed, like "fatal," "not compatible with life," and "catastrophic diagnosis." Stunned, she listened and stoically took notes on the referrals for a maternal fetal medicine specialist and pediatric cardiologist.

Trisomy 18, or Edwards Syndrome, is a genetic condition that causes severe physical growth delays during fetal development. The condition is usually fatal pre-term, with only a small percentage of children living a few days or weeks outside of the womb. Most babies are either stillborn or miscarried.

Rarely, a child with Trisomy 18 may survive about a year. The condition occurs when a person has an extra copy of chromosome 18, which is random and unpredictable. The children are severely underdeveloped and often have low birth weights, severely limited mental development, and aggressive - and usually fatal – heart and respiratory issues. There is no cure for Trisomy 18.

Later that afternoon, with so many emotions swirling, the Freaufs discovered the gender of their baby from a pre-arranged reveal from cupcakes made by friends. Their child was another boy. They began a dizzying round of medical specialist visits and testing the following week.

"We were fortunate that none of our doctors encouraged us to terminate, but it was still a conversation we had to have with each new doctor we met. No matter what, this child was a gift from God, and we wanted to give him the best chance at life. Our trust was fully in God and His plan for this sweet boy even though the outcome was something we would've never chosen," said Lauren.

Small mercies helped Lauren and Ross through this time. They were thankful for family and friends who mobilized to help watch their toddler Wells while they navigated medical visits, and despite the tight regulations of a world gripped with COVID, Ross was allowed to participate in medical appointments.

While most prospective fathers were regulated to FaceTime visits, Ross was allowed to come in a back entrance, masked up, and participate in the prenatal visits.

An initial round of blood tests gave glimpses of hope for a misdiagnosis, or a "lesser" trauma, but the baby's heart was very small, and it was hard to determine heart defects at that time.

"We were trying to navigate that confusing road," said Lauren. "It was a lot to have on our shoulders. I am not a medical person. I don't enjoy medical shows. I'm squeamish and I tried not to Google anything. I had to focus on what was best for our small family."

As word of the diagnosis began to spread amongst their friends and family circles, a few people brought up the organization Abel Speaks, and encouraged Lauren and Ross to reach out. Abel Speaks (www.abelspeaks.org) was formed by Daniel and Kelly Crawford in Dallas, Texas, following a similar diagnosis for their child. Abel Speaks, which now serves families nationwide, provides support for families who have chosen to carry a child with a life-limiting diagnosis. Abel Speaks serves and supports families throughout pregnancy and beyond, with mentorship programs, and by providing medical networking, maternity and birth photography, unique commemorative keepsakes, community family retreats, and memorial service planning.

Lauren was appreciative, but hesitant, to reach out to the organization, still hoping for a miracle. The couple opted for an amniocentesis at 18 weeks to get a definitive diagnosis, which confirmed their worst fear of Trisomy 18.

"There was so much crying. It was so hard," Lauren admitted. "I had my dark moments of staying in bed a lot, but at the same time, I tried to not dwell there. In July, I had committed to walking a mile a day with Wells. It's probably one of the silliest decisions I made in a Texas summer, but the fresh air and exercise, even in the hot air, was what my mental health needed.

We were in a tailspin of dealing with the diagnosis, finding a new doctor and hospital with a critical care NICU, and then just constantly having to tell everyone what was going on, over and over. It was emotionally draining."

"But you know," she added, "Worrying is like a rocking chair. It's something to do, but it gets you nowhere."

Ross and Lauren decided to reach out to Abel Speaks. They were assigned a "mentor couple," Blake and Lindsey, who had lost their daughter, Elizabeth Joy, a year and a half prior. The Freaufs were quickly wrapped in a community that chose joy during sorrow.

They were encouraged to savor the moments of pregnancy and celebrate whatever time they had with their boy. "Just having someone who's walked that road before who could guide us was so helpful. They would say, hey, what you're thinking is totally normal; you're doing all the right things. We were incredibly thankful for that advice," Lauren said, "because it inspired us to take a road trip with the baby to visit the Ouachita National Forest and we cherished even the small things like going to the playground with his big brother."

It was hard to talk with Wells about the baby, Lauren added. "He was seeing my belly grow, but at two years old, he didn't really understand pregnancy. It was even harder for him to comprehend that his brother, who he hadn't met yet, was sick."

Abel Speaks encouraged the family to name their baby. "We understood people wanted to know our son for himself and not by his diagnosis," Lauren explained. "We just didn't know what his name was yet. We knew we wanted something a little biblically stronger for this child, because we knew there was a story that God was writing that we were just helping to facilitate."

"People would ask if they could pray for us and then they'd ask his name. When we read the name Ezra and its Hebrew meaning of "helper," we immediately knew that was his name. Through all of this, Ross and I felt our marriage and faith getting stronger. It was an incredible feeling to think that Ezra was helping strengthen that. We knew somehow, and in some way, Ezra was going to help people. We just didn't know how. And we may never know how. It felt right."

Their focus shifted to enjoying what time they had with Ezra. Beyond day-to-day moments, they mixed in special travel and play, and of course, many doctor visits.

"We wondered how long we'd have Ezra," Lauren said, noting that doctors warned she could have a miscarriage at any moment all the way to term. "We had to decide what we were going to do for the next few months. Did we want to fly all over the country and find doctors to do interventions and try to prolong Ezra's life? Did we choose comfort care, where you just love on the child for as much time as you have? There was a good chance he would be born with serious heart issues. Did I want to put him through immediate heart surgery and risk losing him on an operating table, or did I want him to be wrapped in our arms when he passed?"

The terror of Trisomy 18 is that babies "present" in many ways. They may be stillborn, and all will have some combination of serious medical conditions. Yet, some babies live hours, if not weeks or months. Some Abel Speaks families were able to be with their child up to two years. The list of "what ifs" is terrifying for families.

"We were extremely fortunate that our maternal fetal medicine physician and pediatric cardiologist granted Ross an exception to be in the exam rooms," Lauren said. "The sonograms we had on Ezra will always hold a special place in our hearts because those were the only times we would hear sweet Ezra's heartbeat and I am so thankful we could be together for that."

The seasons began to change, and Lauren and Ross knew a change was headed their way as well.

Travel in nature and through national parks always brought them happiness, so they headed for a favorite spot in Hot Springs, Arkansas at Lake Hamilton. Able Speaks gifted them a family maternity photo shoot. The cherished moments knowing Ezra was a part of those quiet, happy times as a family helped them plan for the uncertain future and Lauren's December due date.

While the world was wrapped in the drama of the November 2020 presidential election, Lauren began struggling with high blood pressure, headaches, and high amniotic fluid. Doctor visits became more frequent and during what she felt was a routine check-up, the on-call OBGYN for her practice admitted her to the hospital for observation and testing. Lauren had developed preeclampsia, a dangerous pregnancy complication for the mother, which could lead to excessive high blood pressure, dangerous swelling, and strokes.

Lauren had transferred to a new OBGYN practice and was anxious to have her physician by her side for the upcoming difficult journey. However, her doctor had contracted COVID-19, and an on-call physician arrived. Two things happened, Lauren said. "My doctor's name is Dr. Angela Angel, and I looked at the chart in labor and delivery and saw it said, 'Freauf Angel.' You can't make this up. I took a picture of that."

Her on-call physician, Dr. Marianne Ebrahim, was exactly who they needed that weekend. Lauren said, "During such a traumatic and devastating time, she was the light we needed. She made us laugh throughout the weekend and kept us calm. I told Ross I couldn't decide if I wanted her to be my doctor or my friend. It was the first time we had met her, and we were very thankful that I was where I needed to be to get the medical care that I needed."

Lauren had hoped to spend a little time in the hospital to stabilize, and then go home for the month to come, but that didn't happen. Tests showed severe preeclampsia. Lauren's mother, brother, and sister-in-law booked red-eye flights from Kentucky and California to be with them, and Lauren was induced on that Saturday night.

Labor was slow and the hours ticked by through Sunday and into Monday morning, November 9. Dr. Ebrahim was off her on-call time, but told Lauren, "I'm sticking with you."

As they talked, Lauren sensed she was about to give birth. At 5:19 a.m., a test showed Ezra's heartbeat was slowing. At 5:27 a.m., Ezra Hayes Freauf was born "sleeping" or stillborn.

"What followed was the hardest day of our lives," Lauren said through tears. "The medical team was so gracious and took some photos for us. We had several private hours with Ezra, and our gathered family were able to spend a few moments each with us."

Ezra was swaddled in a blanket that was embroidered with the phrase, 'All we have is now.'

"We had indescribable peace throughout the pregnancy because we felt there was a lesson in what was to come. There was peace in the sense of he's not in pain, he's not suffering, he's not struggling, but the time in the delivery room was overwhelmingly sad," admitted Lauren.

Leaving the hospital on that Tuesday empty handed was devastating. "It was surreal," Lauren said. "I came home and went straight to bed for several days."

Together, as a family, they moved forward, day-by-day. They treasured the special gift of an "Ezra Bear" stuffed animal that has a recording of Ezra's heartbeat sewn inside. Friends, family, therapists, and Abel Speaks supported them, as days became months. Lauren's mother stayed with them for seven weeks, which helped them with the recovery and grieving process. Wells, now four years old, learns each day a bit more about the journey his brother led them on.

That's where Abel Speaks has been a "godsend" for the family. The connections and friendships made have filled a difficult time with hope. "When I have a rough day, I can text my mentor or several other Abel Speaks parents for support," Lauren explained. "I don't have to dive into the whole backstory; I can be raw and honest and ask a question or just say I need someone to talk with and they will be there."

Ezra still 'speaks' through each day for the Freaufs, as they cherish his memory and move ahead with hope. They have established memorials to Ezra and participate in fundraising and education efforts for Abel Speaks. Lauren and Ross have become mentors for other families traveling this difficult road.

"We walked with our first couple over the summer and their little girl was born at the end of August. She lived just under 24 hours," Lauren said. "You hate to see another family going through this, but to be able to connect with them and be a support, it's just been kind of beautiful to see and to connect with them on that."

It's not something you just put in the past, Lauren said. "These children still speak – to our hearts and lives – and the more we say their names, the more they remain in our world. This was a life that was lost, but it is a life that should be celebrated."

She plans to keep working with Abel Speaks through different channels to give back gratitude for the help they provided her family. As time goes on and they prepare to mark what would be Ezra's second birthday, the family reflects on the future, hoping to grow their family again at some point.

"I sometimes feel like God is sitting back and saying, 'Just wait, I have more good things in store for you,'" Lauren said. "We are focusing on Wells and using Ezra's life as a teaching moment, because that's been a big part of Wells' short four years on Earth."

Lauren laughed. "It's the little things. Ezra was cremated, and we have him in this beautiful wooden box on our mantle, with a canvas of his name that Able Speaks gave us, that hangs over the box. One day, Ross and Wells were playing and throwing a football back and forth inside the house. I was in the other room and heard something fall. I thought, boys will be boys."

"Then, I heard Ross say, 'You knocked your brother off the mantle.' I had an immediate flash to the scene in the movie *Meet the Parents* that is so funny and awful at once, but thankfully, all was well with Ezra. Later, Ross and I were able to look at that as a beautiful moment as if Ezra were here. They'd be brothers, there would be bruises, there would be cuts, there would be all this stuff. We would say it was like brothers being brothers, knocking each other around."

"We are still a grieving family, but we have hope for the future. We know there is so much more joy to come for our family. Who knows what each new day will bring? Whatever it will be, it will be beautiful.

And Ezra will speak and be on our hearts forever."

WHITNEY STRONG

WHITNEY AUSTIN

"I've got to live. I've got to get home to my children."

September 6, 2018, changed Whitney Austin's life forever. Before the workday even began, a beautiful fall morning darkened to a hellish landscape when she walked into the midst of a mass shooting at the Fifth Third Bank Center on Fountain Square, in Cincinnati, Ohio.

As she faced the wrath of a madman, Omar Enrique Santa Perez, she laid on the ground, shot multiple times. Her mind raced to facets of her life. Her family. Her children. Her husband. Her job. Her memories.

"My life was not supposed to end this way," Whitney Austin said.

Whitney didn't aspire to work in banking. She graduated with a degree in psychology, but along the way, decided that wasn't what she wanted to pursue. A friend who was a teller at Fifth Third Bank suggested Whitney explore job openings there while she pondered next steps.

She took a job at Fifth Third Bank, and to her surprise, never looked back. She quickly moved up the ranks there, to Vice President, Digital Lending Product Manager, and was happily based mostly at corporate headquarters in Cincinnati, Ohio, 15 years later.

She and her family left their home of Louisville, Kentucky in 2014 so her husband, Waller, could obtain a master's degree in fine arts. They lived in both Chicago and St. Louis, while Whitney traveled nationwide for her job with Fifth Third Bank. She was thrilled when they returned to Louisville in 2017, which made her commute to Cincinnati under a two-hour drive. She still spent several days a week in Cincinnati, so she also maintained an apartment there.

About a month before the shooting, the Austin family decided to purchase a home in Louisville. Given all the details purchasing a home and orchestrating a move entails, Whitney curtailed her trips to Cincinnati for a bit. "It was nice to take a bit of a break and spend more time with my family to concentrate on purchasing our new house," Whitney said. Plus, life in general, with active five and seven-year-old children, who were involved in play dates, school, and sports, was a happy mix of chaos.

The Thursday after Labor Day was a typical busy morning for the Austin family. "We were all rushing around," Whitney remembered. "I had to get to Cincinnati. The kids had to get to school. My husband was taking care of our children, and they were so sweet and wanted me to give them multiple kisses before I left. They wanted mommy to stay home. I assured them I'd be home that evening and all would be well."

Whitney hit the road for the drive up I-71, listened to a podcast, checked in by phone with some colleagues, and as she was arriving, joined a scheduled conference call. As she was coming out of the parking garage, she paused at the crosswalk, cautious that cars often ignore that crossing.

"I was worried about that," she explained. "I expected that to be my 'worry' for the morning. I didn't really notice that the plaza was empty. It was an important conference call, so I was focused on that."

It was a normal morning. Until it wasn't, seconds later.

Whitney recalled the horror she faced. "When I walked up to the building, I noticed that the glass in the revolving door that I used to enter the building was shattered, but the door was still attached. I thought that was weird, someone must have thrown a rock at the door."

It wasn't a rock. It was a bullet. Whitney walked into the hell created by the mass shooter.

"As soon as I pushed on the revolving door, I was hit by the first barrage of bullets, and I collapsed right there in the middle of that revolving door. I immediately began to assess my situation. What was happening to me? I remember feeling a burning sensation across my upper body and thinking, well, nobody's right next to me. No one is stabbing me. It must be that I'm getting shot."

But why? Her mind leapt to the thought it could be a mass shooting. Survival mode kicked in instantly.

"I had to survive for my children," she said. "I tried to get up but couldn't because I was too weak. I looked out onto the square and saw there wasn't anyone there to save me. I tried to reach my phone to dial 911, but my arm was too badly injured to move."

And then, the second barrage of bullets hit.

She realized the shooter, who she couldn't see, was watching her move, so as hard and terrifying as it was, instinct kicked in and she decided to play dead. It was a chilling moment for Whitney.

"I thought, this is it. I'm dead," she explained. "I started praying and concentrating on being still. It had been exactly one minute of my life, and I thought my life was over. I didn't want to die."

At that moment, the Cincinnati police arrived on the scene. She saw officer Alphonso Staples approaching and started shouting, "I have a five- and seven-year-old! You have to save me!"

In the chaos of the moment, she was confused when officer Staples told her to play dead and be quiet. She didn't realize he could see the shooter and was trying to protect her from a third round of bullets. He also was confused, thinking Whitney's children were on the scene somewhere.

"In that life and death moment, all I could think about was my children would be motherless," Whitney said. "I needed to tell someone, anyone that. I needed to live. I didn't realize that all the officers were quickly taking care of the situation."

The Cincinnati police had recently undergone active shooter training and were primed for the situation. They arrived quickly, assessed the situation, ultimately killed the shooter, and feverishly attended to the victims. Three people, Pruthvi Raj Kandepi, Richard Newcomer, and Luis Felipe Calderón, were dead. Whitney and Brian Sarver were injured and fighting for their survival. Santa Perez fired a total of 35 rounds before being shot dead by an officer. He had hundreds of rounds in his possession.

"They just did everything correctly," Whitney explained. "They pulled me out of the revolving door and immediately put a tourniquet on me. I don't remember it, but I've seen video of them helping me walk out, because from my belly button down, the only bullet that hit me below just skimmed my left foot."

Whitney had lived, but she was severely injured. She passed out and when she woke up in the hospital, she was told she had been shot twelve times. Miraculously, none of the bullets hit a major organ or artery. Several bullets went across her chest and breasts, and more lodged in both arms. "Along the right side of my body, I still have hundreds, if not thousands, of tiny pieces of shrapnel in my body," Whitney said.

Her long road to recovery began. But she was alive. Gloriously alive.

"I have this huge well of gratitude that not only did I live, but I got back to my husband and those kids who I told everyone about on my way to the hospital, so they would make sure that they did their best to help me survive. The most significant damage was to my arms," she added. "I've had four surgeries to repair bones and nerve damage and reattach tendons. When you think about the thousands of things that went right for me that day, there's just no explanation to the question of 'Why me?'" she added.

"I don't subscribe to the theory that God is out there choosing winners and losers. I lived. Others didn't. I got back to my husband and children, and my parents, and my sister, and my friends. That just kind of kicks me in the butt and says, you can walk out that door today, you can make that speech, you can talk to that person because it's a responsibility that you have now. I was given that gift, and knew I had to do something with it."

Whitney said that was an entirely different concept of who she was previously. "Gratitude and hope inspire me to do hard things," she said. "As instinctual as it was to fight to live for my kids, it was just as instinctual to honor the gift of life and pay it forward."

Just a week into her recovery, Whitney and Waller were talking about the shooting and her next steps. She knew she had to take action of some sort. They decided to create the Whitney|Strong organization, which would be focused on finding common ground to end gun violence through data-driven, responsible gun ownership solutions.

"We knew we didn't want to be like some groups out there, who are viewed as anti-gun or following a particular political stripe," she said. "We wanted to include gun owners on both sides of the political aisle. Nobody should be OK with unsafe communities."

As she began her arduous recovery, which stretched over the next ten months, she took the time to form a board of directors and even obtain a license from the Secretary of State's office to make Whitney|Strong an official nonprofit organization. Whitney was grateful for the assistance of friends and colleagues who helped it all come together.

"I couldn't use my hands for anything," she laughed. "I couldn't pull up my pants, much less design a website or text instructions to people. There were so many people who were willing to help me and introduce me to the team that got the work done for me."

Strangers and friends supported the family in day-to-day efforts as well. "Every day, someone was at my house with a meal, or driving my kids around, or bringing them gifts," she explained. "It was always, 'How can we help you?' My cousin moved in and lived with us full time for 45 days. It gave me the time and support to start healing physically and mentally, as I worked with physical therapists, occupational therapists, and my psychiatrist. I received so much more support than any one person deserves, but we were so thankful."

As the months went by, Whitney found her voice and her strength in Whitney|Strong. She had long thought about volunteering for a similar organization, particularly following the Sandy Hook tragedy.

"I kept thinking, none of this is acceptable for my kids," Whitney said. "This isn't the country or life or world that I want them to inherit. It took up a lot of space in my head. One of the thoughts I had when I was being shot was how dare I always think I was immune to this violence. This can happen anywhere, to anyone, and it certainly was happening to me in that moment. Secondly, if I survived, I knew I would have to make this my life's work."

She paused and added, "Every time someone dies from gun violence, I am reminded that I lived. I must be a part of the solution."

Whitney|Strong is now a national, non-partisan organization that is focused on responsible gun ownership and ending gun violence. It works to lobby legislators, educate the public, and act on data to implement educational opportunities. Funding research to find science-based steps to reverse gun violence is a key component also. Whitney|Strong is made up of gun violence survivors, gun owners, and advocates who are concerned about the lives lost to all forms of gun violence.

As she grows Whitney|Strong, she is conscious of growing her personal healing too. Whitney has worked over the ensuing years to regain strength and usage of her hands and arms, but nerve damage still makes certain movements painful and difficult. Her broken bones have healed and she's able to do most movements but there is a significant difference in her strength. She also struggles with supination, in turning her palms to face up or down, for example.

The nerve damage is something she can live with, but certainly, wishes wasn't an issue. Her future though, remains uncertain. "The thing is," Whitney said, "the future is unknown when you have thousands of pieces of shrapnel scattered throughout your body. There is a lot that could happen."

She had back surgery earlier in 2022 for an issue that was difficult to diagnose. "Because an MRI involves heat, it could heat up the shrapnel and make it move and obviously, create more damage," Whitney said.

She had to wait an extended period for insurance to approve a specialized MRI that would work on her body. "The shooting has created a domino effect on my body that will affect my life from now on."

The emotional toll is a daily challenge also. "Other people died that day," she said quietly. "Why did I live? I deal with a lot of anxiety. I worry I, or someone I love, could be caught up in another mass shooting. I have to relive the shooting often in speeches, meetings, and interviews and that also stirs up emotions."

Whitney|Strong has become a calling, with Whitney leading the organization full time since May 2019. It's on her mind continually, which can still be difficult with young children. "They understand the gift that we were given and that we have a responsibility now to help reduce gun violence in this country," she said, adding, "I am both realistic and hopeful. Gun violence doesn't discriminate, it touches all of us. You have to talk with everyone and get different perspectives in order to reach the best solution possible. That's just the reality of this topic."

Since its founding, Whitney|Strong has worked on several responsible gun ownership solutions, including securing the first hearing on gun safety legislation in the Kentucky legislature in over a decade.

Whitney and her team joined Ohio Governor Mike DeWine to announce the STRONG Ohio legislation following the Dayton Oregon district shooting in 2019. The organization has distributed over 12,000 gun locks across Kentucky and Ohio, thanks to a partnership with the American Academy of Pediatrics and with the support of the National Shooting Sports Foundation. They've trained over 500 people in ways to reduce gun violence in neighborhoods disproportionately impacted by gun violence, and importantly, lobbied Senators Mitch McConnell (KY) and Robert Portman (OH) to ensure passage of the federal Bipartisan Safer Communities Act in 2022.

The Bipartisan Safer Communities Act implemented several changes affecting the mental health system, school safety programs and gun safety laws. This included extended background checks for gun purchasers under the age of 21, clarification of federal firearms licensing requirements, funding for state red flag laws, and other crisis intervention programs, and more. Whitney and her entire family were in the Senate gallery to witness the historic legislation pass. She and her Whitney|Strong team had lobbied lawmakers heavily throughout the process.

She wrote in her blog, "There is nothing like being in D.C. to advocate for the cause you hold dear. It is the honor of my life to represent your voice to these members and staff as we push for new laws that will keep us safe. Before the speeches and votes, Senator McConnell made his way up to the gallery to greet us. I felt so deeply tied to the outcome that I needed reassurance that the bill would pass. He gave me that reassurance and I thanked him for his leadership. I was so overcome with gratitude I asked if I could give him a hug. I'm not sure that happens very often, but when one of the most powerful men in the history of the U.S. decides to do the right thing on the issue I hold so dear, how could I not be overcome with gratitude?

As the final vote came in and the vote total was announced, I was overcome with absolute pure joy! This thing that everyone said would never happen; this thing that I had given up my career for and had put my hopes and beliefs into; this thing that had to happen so that everything after it felt more doable; it was the single most joyful moment of my professional life."

But, fresh off that success, she knows there is much more work to do. "I'm also realistic in that I know this journey will take a long time, especially when one of our key measures of success is policy and legislative work," she said.

"We are so proud to be the only organization in the country that has a bill with bipartisan support that is focused on reducing mass violence and suicide. What that really boils down to is someone was injured or killed, and the tool used to complete the act was a gun. So, whether it's suicide that was completed with a gun, or interpersonal violence, or an accident, or a mass shooting, or a stray bullet fired into the community - that is all gun violence. And, if you view it in that way, you're talking about more than 40,000 people dying a year, which is on par with the number of people dying each year of breast cancer or in automobile accidents. It's a substantial number."

"It is really important to help people understand how large the number is," she continued. "We can do better if we can all see common ground and consider the viewpoints of others. I'm fully aware that it is going to take some time to make change, particularly on policy within states like Kentucky and Ohio. But, I'm also very hopeful because there are so many moments along the way where there is a small crack in building the dam."

For more than two decades, beginning in the late 1990s, Whitney said, Congress did not fund gun violence research. That cooling effect on gun violence research funding impacted policies and legislation for decades. When Congress finally appropriated $25 million in 2019 in research funding to the CDC to study gun violence, Whitney felt hopeful once again. "It's amazingly hopeful, because not only is the government back in the business of research, but both sides of the aisle came together to do this."

"And this was the point Republicans were still in the majority in the Senate and had previously said no to any gun control legislation that came from the House," she added. "But this time, the Senate did not get in the way of appropriating those funds. It was a really huge moment. Whenever I see a change in Congress, or in a big corporation sponsoring a gun control event, that's an example of change coming."

That change, she said, is a moment for hope. "When I have more emails into Congress and state legislatures than the year prior, that's a moment of hope. It's tough when people won't schedule meetings with you. It's tough for me, as a victim of gun violence, to be knee deep in data every day about the number of people injured or killed by gun violence. But still, I hope.

I hate, as a mother, when I read stories about 15-year-old kids dying by gun violence. I feel for those mothers, and those stories always get to me. I have a lot of really difficult moments, but then there are helpful moments, and victories in changing minds."

Whitney Austin never asked for this life's work. She became a victim in 2018 but didn't let that crush her spirit. She knew she had a mission to fulfill. "It's important to me that everybody really understands how broad gun violence is in all of its forms," she concluded. "There's got to be something within all of us that we care about more than the other person for whatever reason. We have a responsibility to make change in the world. I always return to my gratitude for living that September day.

I find it addictive and intoxicating, this hope, because there is just enough of it sprinkled along the way to keep you going every day. Every day…is precious."

BOWTIES AND BUTTERFLIES

REMEMBERING CHARLES GANT

In late May 2009, a week before school let out for the summer, the Gant family was running full tilt on life. Mom Kelly and dad Lenny Gant were busy with work, and even busier managing life with their three young sons. Life was good and the summer was beckoning. Son Owen was ten and in fourth grade. Charles was eight and in second grade. Their youngest, Campbell, was learning the ropes in a four-year-old preschool program.

As the school year drew to a close, Charles started feeling unwell. He had a fever, sore throat, and was a bit achy. Kelly took him to the doctor, thinking he might have strep throat, but they dismissed his symptoms as a typical virus. After a few days of TLC, Charles improved, but then later, he began feeling bad again. They returned to the doctor that following Friday. As he rested on Saturday, Kelly and her husband attended a wedding. Their long-time babysitter called them at the wedding, concerned that Charles was vomiting and asking for his parents.

The Gants returned home quickly and Charles' grandfather, who is a physician, came over to check on his grandson. He tested Charles for signs of meningitis, but he did not have the right symptoms. He didn't improve overnight, so early the next morning, the Gants took their son to the pediatrician again. His tests were also inconclusive, but he recommended they visit the local children's hospital to get IV fluids for Charles.

"The ER at Norton Children's Hospital (in Louisville, Kentucky) admitted him, and that night, he was just not himself," said Kelly. "He was hallucinating, and a later CT scan on Monday showed his brain was swelling. They moved us to the pediatric intensive care unit, so we knew he'd have their full attention."

The doctors still weren't sure what was happening with Charles and suggested that one parent go home to get some rest, as they might be in for a long stretch. Kelly went home to rest a bit but returned quickly when further testing showed little to no brain activity due to the swelling. The doctors were trying everything possible to help Charles, but it soon became clear that he would not survive.

The Gants were faced with a horrifying reality. In the space of only a few days, their happy, healthy young son was not going to live to see the end of another week.

"Despite all our prayers, we knew the logical and scientific side of it all meant we would have to take him off of life support," said Kelly. "We were in total shock at that point. I don't think I could even cry; it was just too surreal. There were dozens of people at the hospital to visit and support us, which wouldn't happen today post-COVID, and there was just so much activity.

We had someone bring Owen and Campbell to the hospital, and my parents were already there. Lenny's parents were on the way. The hospital sent an art therapist to us who took pictures of Charles on life support so she could sit down with the boys to explain everything to them before they saw him. She stayed with us in the room and had the boys make art to remember Charles by. She helped prepare them to say goodbye to their brother."

On Wednesday, doctors determined a rare and violent form of viral encephalitis was attacking Charles' body. "He passed away on Wednesday, June 3, 2009, which was the last day of school for the year," said Kelly. Charles was removed from life support and passed in about 20 minutes. The nurses made molds of his hands and the family was able to spend quiet time together at the end of Charles' all-too-short life.

Family, friends, and their school family wrapped the Gants in love and support. "His service was that Saturday, and hundreds of people attended," explained Kelly. "There were so many children and parents, and people from all parts of our lives there. The nurses who cared for him were like family by that point. They were there,

24 hours a day, caring for him and taking care of our family."

The outpouring of grief and support helped the family, but they existed in a stunned fog. "It's not an easy thing to ask for help in any situation, but when you're in something as overwhelming as this, every moment can freeze you," Kelly explained. "People all want to help, but they don't know what to do or say also. You can only accept so many casseroles."

Kelly and Lenny felt blessed by close friends who had children the same ages as theirs, who took over "kid duty" for a while as they fought to find a new normal. Thankfully, as a teacher, Kelly was already off for the summer, so that time was precious to her to not have the additional worry of her job at that time. "We were able to be together during that summer and not have to be anywhere," she said.

The family began therapy to help make sense of their tragic loss. Owen and Campbell were so young it was difficult to understand and manage their grief. Therapy helped move the family forward day by day. It wasn't just a thing to do for a few weeks – the Gant family has worked on healing from their tragedy for years.

Realizing that everyone grieves differently, the Gants were cautious to honor each other's needs and feelings throughout that most difficult summer and beyond. Collectively, they all agreed that they felt a need to give back gratitude – and funding – to the hospital and professionals who worked tirelessly to try and save Charles' life.

"It was how we sought hope," Kelly said.

Kelly and Lenny talked with the children's hospital foundation on how to best honor Charles' memory and the dedicated work of the doctors and staff who cared for him. Since his diagnosis of viral encephalitis was not a "traditional" giving category – like cancer, or diabetes, for example – it was suggested that the Gants create a specific event tied to raising awareness for the disease, or as a way to remember Charles. After much thought, the family created the Bourbon & Bowties fundraising event to benefit the Norton Children's Hospital.

Bourbon & Bowties combined all the elements and more of a festive southern evening: great food prepared by local notable chefs, a bucolic setting on an area farm, lots of live and silent auction items, and of course, Kentucky bourbon. Southern casual attire – including fun bowties – heralded a more relaxed setting than a traditional black-tie event. The event was an immediate hit and sold out quickly.

The money raised went back to the hospital's Child Life and Expressive Art Therapy department. As they did for the Gant family, therapists based in the hospital help families manage stressful hospital experiences through art, puppetry, writing and drama. Families and patients work to express their fears and dreams while externalizing their energy, which allows their bodies to heal. Music therapists in the department address physical, psychological, and social functions through music-related activities, which help improve pain relief, sleep, and appetite.

"It was so important to us how they handled our situation and helped our boys, so we wanted to give back to the program," added Kelly.

The following year, the Gants decided to honor a different child each year who faced a personal medical battle. "My husband wears bowties a lot, so the first year of the event we designed a bowtie in memory of Charles that had frogs and dragonflies on it, because that's what he loved," Kelly said. "So, every year now, each honoree's family designs a signature bow tie with Vineyard Vines, which helps them represent their child's interests on the design."

Children honored face issues like cancer, heart defects, premature birth, and various life-threatening issues. While always keeping the memory of Charles Gant alive, the event has honored the following children: Laurel Dortch, Maxwell W. Johnson, Owen McMasters, Anna-Maria Beck, Clara and Wilson McGarvey, Tanner Demling, Mason Christensen, Mya White, Hazel Leggett, and Jonathan Young.

"We celebrated our tenth event in 2019, and honored all the children from the past years, as well as Chef Dean Corbett, who helped us host and begin the event, but who sadly passed away recently," said Kelly.

Bourbon & Bowties has sold out several years in a row. After a short break due to COVID-19, the 2022 event was an enormous success, netting $338,823 going directly to helping children and families served by Norton Children's Hospital in Louisville. Since the event's inception, the community has contributed more than $2.3 million, benefitting nearly 185,000 children annually in Kentucky and Southern Indiana.

The event helps the Gants keep Charles front and center in many minds, and it brings peace and hope to emerge from the sadness. "My husband and I look forward to the event every year," Kelly said. "While it makes us sad to relive Charles' death each time, it also makes us happy to see all the good that comes from the event. Meeting the honorees and their families every year is so important to us."

Over the years, both Owen and Campbell have participated in the teen volunteer program at Norton Children's Hospital in the summertime and served on the hospital's teen board. "Owen is now 22 years old and Campbell is 17, and they've begun attending the event recently as well," she added. "It's built in them a knowledge and desire to help others and reach out to do charitable work. They see the event results and are so proud that our family has done something to help others, all in Charles' memory."

Grief, Kelly said, can either drive you apart or drive you closer together. While it's a club no one wants to enter, she feels her family has done the best they could to claw towards the light. "We focused on our family," she explained. "We share our story, and even though it is painful, as time goes by, you realize that sharing our grief, and keeping Charles' memory present, helps not only our family, but others who might be in similar terrible circumstances."

It's okay to laugh, she said, as much as it is okay to cry. There's always that moment, that glimpse, that memory that creeps in and generates either joy or sadness. Those feelings should be honored in the moment and shared, not buried.

"You may think you're okay, but it's also important to realize when you are not," Kelly said. "Ask a friend for help. Talk to someone, whether it's your spouse, a friend, or a therapist. Cry when you need to. Rage at the realization you've suffered this tragedy. All those feelings are perfectly normal and need to be released."

Every time Charles' birthday rolls around, the Gants make cupcakes and gather as a family for a meal. They may visit his graveside or plan an outing together. They always meet, even years later, to honor the spirit of that vivacious eight-year-old boy.

Kelly paused. "I still see some of his friends and their parents, so it's always nice to see those kids now, but it's bittersweet because I do wonder, what would Charles look like and what would he be doing? He'd be a junior in college this year. It's heartwarming to hear from his old classmates, but it's also sad."

As her husband Lenny often says, grief is a very deep cut. Each layer gets a little better and less painful over time, but the scar always remains.

"For anyone grieving, life goes on, because that's just what happens," Kelly explained. "You can be in a dark place, but the day-to-day moments of life still happen. As years pass, I feel like I can talk about Charles more easily. The raw pain isn't there as much, but it never goes away completely. You just learn how to live around this new life."

The Gant family continues to honor Charles with philanthropy beyond Bourbon & Bowties. "We find hope by being able to give back to others in Charles' name," she added. "We try to show others that even though we've been through such a horrible event, we have been able to find hope by helping others."

As a pre-school and kindergarten teacher, Kelly decided to further honor Charles by starting a memorial scholarship program at her school where she teaches, Second Presbyterian Weekday School in Louisville. As the school has a philosophy of outdoor and play-based learning, Kelly purchased boots for the children to play outside.

"Charles loved frogs and butterflies, so I purchased boots decorated with frogs on them," Kelly laughed. "Children can wear the boots and jump in muddy puddles all day if they want. Charles would certainly have jumped in any puddle he could find, and he loved his time as a student at Second Pres. It's a small, happy way we keep his memory out there."

Charles loved "all critters" she added, particularly butterflies. "I always say, hope is a butterfly. At his service, some of my best friends released butterflies and that is an image I always carry. Every time I see a butterfly now, I think of Charles. I know he's out there, looking after us, and it makes me smile."

"Hope," she concluded quietly. "Hope is a butterfly in the sunshine."

YOUR HOPEFUL LIFE

My friend April Johnson-Stearns founded a magazine named *Wildfire* in 2015 that serves the younger breast cancer community. It is full of personal narratives on different aspects of cancer survivorship. I encourage you to visit her website at *Wildfire Magazine*, wildfirecommunity.org. April says, "I firmly believe everyone has a story to tell, but I discovered through *Wildfire* that not everyone feels their story is worthy or knows where to begin in putting pen to paper. Many people -- maybe yourself included -- have been telling themselves a story for years that they are not a writer. Their story doesn't matter. I'm here to tell you otherwise."

I submitted poetry to *Wildfire* in the past and when I had the idea for this book, I asked April to help coach me on telling some of my stories. I also asked her to help include a section of journal prompts so that readers could discover for themselves how to have hope in even the hardest of times.

April told me, "Memoirs are powerful to us, and not because we want to know all the details of everything that happened to someone. Rather, we want to know what happened next: How did they go on afterward? How did they make sense of those events? How did they find acceptance and peace and, yes, hope?"

I'm so grateful for April's help with this section, "Your Hopeful Life." Collaborating with her helped me see that powerful stories are within all of us. I share here April's wishes for you as you work through this section and find your story.

"The reason we read and absorb stories from others is because they contain the same questions that reside within all of us. We want to know how to go on after difficult events. We want to know what it all means. We want to know how to find peace," says April.

"Now it's your turn. It's time to tune into your inner writer to use writing to access the questions that burn within you -- and the answers that are there, too."

Dear Reader,

The instructions are simple. Anyone can do it. Your Hopeful Life is made up of writing prompts and life prompts. Flow between them as you wish. Find a quiet place where you can be uninterrupted for a period of time. Say, 10 minutes. You can work through the prompts in order or take them as they appeal to you.

Just do. Just write; let whatever wants to come out of you flow uninhibited. Don't edit yourself or worry that you aren't doing it right. Tap into a subconscious flow of thought and just get it down (there is plenty of time to edit later).

The main thing to understand is that there is no right or wrong answer to a prompt. The prompt is just to get you going. See where it takes you and what needs to come out. Congratulations, you're on your way to living a hopeful life!

THE WORKBOOK

~~~~~~

~~~~~~

~~~~~~

~~~~~~

~~~~~~

~~~~~~

HINT *This can be your physical location or your emotional state of mind. Zoom way in, and then slowly zoom out, step by step to reveal where you are writing from.*

"There it is- life, joy, accomplishment. And - lurking in the shadows - fear. But, you have to dive down. Take the risk, live the life, have the adventure. Because if you don't all that's left is fear. A life wrecked in fear is a life only half lived. Dive down!"

TWENTY THINGS THAT MAKE ME SMILE...

☺ _____

☺ _____

☺ _____

☺ _____

☺ _____

☺ _____

☺ _____

☺ _____

☺ _____

☺ _____

☺ _____

☺ _____

☺ _____

☺ _____

☺ _____

☺ _____

☺ _____

☺ _____

☺ _____

☺ _____

SEND A WORD OF GRATITUDE TO SOMEONE YOU LOVE

Take a moment. Find a piece of paper or a card and write a note of appreciation to someone who makes a difference in your life. So often we speed through life without acknowledging the impact we have on each other. Ok, ok... you can also do this in a text or email if that means it will happen. The important part is you take time to share how much they mean to you. Reach out, connect.

NOT SURE WHAT TO SAY? TRY THIS.

Thank you for your steadfast friendship. Through all the ups and downs in life I know I can always turn to you for support, love, encouragement or a swift kick in the rear. My life is richer because of you. I love you.

ONE THING I KNOW NOW THAT I DIDN'T KNOW BEFORE...

(insert a major experience in your life)

THE BEST MONEY I EVER SPENT WAS ON...

AM I GOOD ENOUGH...?

_____

_____

_____

_____

_____

_____

LIFE PROMPT

DO SOMETHING THAT BRINGS YOU JOY

When was the last time you made a decision based on joy? I have a strategy called a "joy filter." When deciding to do something or choose between two things I run it through the joy filter. If it doesn't bring me joy I stop and think if it's worth it. We need more joy in our lives - try it!

A LIST OF THINGS THAT BRING ME JOY THAT I CAN DO ANYTIME, ANY PLACE.

☺ _____

☺ _____

☺ _____

☺ _____

☺ _____

I CARRY WITH ME…

~~~~~~

~~~~~~

~~~~~~

~~~~~~

~~~~~~

~~~~~~

~~~~~~

~~~~~~

~~~~~~

~~~~~~

HINT

It can be really fun to do an inventory of your purse or bag and the significance of the items, but also think about emotional baggage, family legacies, etc. For example, "from my mother I carry with me…"

"That's the thing… you never know what twists and turns lie ahead of you on your journey. It's just the way you face your journey that matters."

Lara

SOAK UP GOLDEN HOUR

Do you know the moment when the sun is setting and the world becomes golden? Some people call this golden hour or magic hour. It is magic. Sometimes it comes and goes so quickly you don't notice it. Try to take a moment in the midst of the magic to take a deep breath and let the radiant sunlight soak into your soul.

CHASE A SUNSET

Have you chased a sunset? Racing to the water's edge to catch the brilliance before the sun sinks below the equator? It's exhilarating. Getting there just in time to plop down, take a deep breath and let the changing sky surround you. I love to swim in the sunset. Diving in the cold crisp water, breaking the surface all you see is the blaze of the sky. Sunsets are a time for reflection on the day past and the day to come. A brilliant bridge between what is past and future. A reminder that even though we can no longer see the sun, it is always there.

"For our lives are made up of each day and each moment. I don't know if I have two years or ten years... but I know I have the day before me." _Lara_

A TIME I DISCOVERED MY OWN STRENGTH...

PLACES/ACTIVITIES IN WHICH I CAN LOSE TRACK OF TIME...

READ A BOOK WITH A CHILD

This is as much about slowing down as it is about reading a good book. Take time to sit on the floor, read the words, giggle, point at the pictures together. It's energizing to see the world through a kiddo's eyes. Might bring some perspective to your own life too.

"Perhaps searching for how to live the most beautiful version of my life is itself the revolution. There isn't a magic moment of clarity where I am going to feel complete peace with my choices, but rather the very act of living the life is what brings the peace" Lara

ACT, DON'T ASK

When you are going through a difficult time many people say, "Let me know how I can help." I guarantee no one is keeping a list of who mentioned this to come back to later with a request. Instead, take the initiative to show love and support without putting the burden on the person you intend to help. Act, don't Ask!

SOME IDEAS OF HOW TO SUPPORT A LOVED ONE, WITHOUT ASKING. YOU CAN COME BACK TO THIS LIST ANYTIME YOU KNOW SOMEONE GOING THROUGH A HARD TIME.

Drop off a gift card for coffee in the mailbox

Rake their leaves, shovel their snow

Plant new plants in their pots

Wash their windows

Set up a regular dog walking time

When you are at the grocery store, send them a text saying "I am going to pick up some staples for you while I am here: toilet paper, coffee, laundry detergent, etc... If you need anything else please let me know."

Add your ideas below and share what worked with others.

A MOMENT I REALIZE I HAD GROWN...

_____

_____

_____

_____

_____

_____

_____

_____

_____

_____

_____

_____

LIFE PROMPT

TAKE CARE OF SOMETHING GREEN

Plants are a fun way to bring life into your home and create intentionality - water them, watch them grow. See how you grow too.

"But, we found a little bit of light in the darkness. We clung to it. And realized that joy and sadness can exist at the same time. Hope and fear." *Lara*

HOPE IS...

A LIST OF SONGS THAT EVOKE A
PARTICULAR TIME AND PLACE IN MY LIFE...

TELL THE STORY OF A SONG FROM YOUR LIST.
WHAT DOES THE SONG BRING TO MIND?
WHY IS IT MEANINGFUL TO YOU?

GET YOUR HAIR WET

So often in life I think we watch because it's just easier. Maybe we don't have a towel, maybe we don't want to do our hair again or the water isn't quite warm enough. But, I promise you I have never regretted jumping in. Let go of things that hold you back. Take the plunge. The invigorating, deep breath you take when you break the surface of the water and realize you did it will be worth it.

JUMP IN!

"We came to understand that when the timeline is shortened, you savor moments even more. We doubled down on hope."

Lara

PART 1: A LIST OF THINGS I'M OBSESSED ABOUT...

GO OUTSIDE
& WATCH THE
CLOUDS

Stop what you are doing. Go outside. Look up. See the clouds drift above you, blowing quickly in the wind or slowly shifting in the light breeze. Lay down flat on your back in the grass. Put your hand on your heart, feel the power of your body beating strongly within. Feel the earth on your back grounding you to this moment. Take a deep breath.

PART 2: A DEEP CONVERSATION WITH MYSELF ABOUT ONE THING FROM MY LIST OF OBSESSIONS...

FOR _____

(your name)

ON _____

(today's date)

TO _____

_____

_____

_____

_____

_____

(that thing you really want to do but haven't let yourself)

SIGNED _____

(your signature)

"We are the authors of our lives. We can't change the fact that cancer invaded our bodies, or that it is killing our friends and tearing apart families. While the tears are still fresh, we can choose what we do next. We turn our heartbreak into action." *Lara*

MY SIDE OF THE STORY: WHAT I HAVEN'T YET TOLD ANYONE IS...

A DESCRIPTION OF A PLACE THAT IS SPECIAL TO ME...

AND A DRAWING OF IT.

WRITE PARTS AND PIECES OF YOURSELF IN THE BUBBLES?

I USED TO BE ...

~~~~~~

~~~~~~

~~~~~~

~~~~~~

~~~~~~

~~~~~~

~~~~~~

AND NOW I AM...

~~~~~~

~~~~~~

~~~~~~

~~~~~~

~~~~~~

~~~~~~

~~~~~~

~~~~~~

~~~~~~

~~~~~~

~~~~~~

WRITE A MANTRA FOR YOURSELF

A MANTRA, GIVEN TO ME BY MY FRIEND EMILY AS SHE DIED OF CANCER:

Everything is working out for my highest good. Out of this situation, only good will come. I am safe.

- LOUISE HAY

WHAT THE WORLD DOESN'T SEE
WHEN THEY LOOK AT ME...

"Approaching life with gratitude
doesn't change your circumstances.
It changes everything." Lara

WRITE A LIST OF THINGS YOU ARE THANKFUL FOR...

☺ ————————————————————————————

☺ ————————————————————————————

☺ ————————————————————————————

☺ ————————————————————————————

☺ ————————————————————————————

☺ ————————————————————————————

☺ ————————————————————————————

☺ ————————————————————————————

☺ ————————————————————————————

☺ ————————————————————————————

☺ ————————————————————————————

☺ ————————————————————————————

☺ ————————————————————————————

☺ ————————————————————————————

☺ ————————————————————————————

☺ ————————————————————————————

☺ ————————————————————————————

DISCOVERING YOURSELF

We are both a work in progress and a masterpiece at the same time.
What are some things you are working on to discover yourself?

- [ ] _____
- [ ] _____
- [ ] _____
- [ ] _____
- [ ] _____
- [ ] _____
- [ ] _____
- [ ] _____
- [ ] _____
- [ ] _____
- [ ] _____
- [ ] _____

THE STORY OF A TIME I WAS EXCEPTIONALLY HAPPY...

> "I've always loved
> a reason to throw
> a party or make
> a toast. Now
> more than ever
> I'm celebrating
> milestones and
> happy moments."
>
> *Lara*

SELF LOVE

Your story is the most powerful part of who you are. Use your authentic voice to tell your own story - starting with how you talk to yourself, beautiful.

DEAR

~~~~~~

~~~~~~

~~~~~~

~~~~~~

[insert hardship]

WHAT HAVE YOU COME TO SHOW ME?

~~~~~~

~~~~~~

~~~~~~

~~~~~~

~~~~~~

~~~~~~

~~~~~~

~~~~~~

HINT *It can be very helpful to write a letter to the issues you face in order to uncover lessons and to shift your perspective from feeling victimized to the role of observer.*

"So, when things don't go your way. When you or someone you love slips up. Pause. (allow yourself to scream & cry if you need to) Take a look at the bigger picture and rally for this one, messy, imperfect life." *Lara*

DO SOMETHING THAT MAKES YOU LAUGH

"There are precious moments of life every day—from a child's hug to laughter with friends. This is what I celebrate. And live for."

THE SECRET OF MY SURVIVAL IS...

_____

_____

_____

_____

_____

_____

_____

_____

_____

_____

_____

we are broken & whole / strong & weak

Hope is not contingent

CONTRIBUTORS

LARA MACGREGOR

FOUNDER, HOPE SCARVES AND A HOPEFUL LIFE

Lara MacGregor was 30 years old and seven months pregnant in 2007 when she was diagnosed with breast cancer. After being gifted headscarves accompanied by a note that said "You can do this" during her treatment, she founded Hope Scarves, which brings hope and community to thousands of people. After seven years in remission, she was diagnosed again, this time with Stage 4 metastatic breast cancer. With her new reality, Lara redefined hope for herself and for her organization as "to live life over cancer." Lara chose to write her story as one of laughter and love and one that embraced every moment intentionally with hope. She called it *A Hopeful Life*. Lara MacGregor passed away peacefully on January 18, 2022. She was just 45 years old.

ANNA LAURA EDWARDS

EXECUTIVE DIRECTOR, HOPE SCARVES

Anna Laura Edwards first met Lara as Bennett MacGregor's preschool teacher. She and Lara became fast friends, and when Lara created Hope Scarves, Anna Laura quickly jumped on board as a volunteer. Later, in 2018, Anna Laura became Hope Scarves' partnership director, working with donor management and facilitating hospital partnerships nationwide. In 2021, Anna Laura was named the first executive director of Hope Scarves, tasked with leading the organization and carrying on Lara's light and legacy.

LAURA ROSS

EXECUTIVE EDITOR AND WRITER

Laura Ross is a nationally published author and public relations professional, who met Lara by chance in 2012 when the firm she worked with provided marketing and public relations assistance to Hope Scarves. Laura and Lara became both friends and colleagues, as Laura continued to manage public and media relations efforts for both Lara and Hope Scarves as it grew in national prominence. Laura also proudly served on the Hope Scarves board of directors for several years.

CONTRIBUTORS

HANNAH SCHILLER

BOOK DESIGNER

Hannah Schiller is a brand designer in Louisville, Kentucky. Her passion lies in working with small businesses, founders, and entrepreneurs to bring their vision to life through branding. Hannah met Lara when she was at the crux of launching her personal brand, My Hopeful Life. Hannah was honored to work with Lara to help actualize her dream.

APRIL STEARNS

WRITER, PART THREE, YOUR HOPEFUL LIFE

April Stearns is the founder and editor-in-chief of *Wildfire Magazine*, the first magazine by and for young women diagnosed with breast cancer. Lara submitted a poem to *Wildfire* years ago and then later, April helped Lara lead a healing writing workshop for Hope Scarves. Lara asked April to help her find her voice and write her own stories. As her book coach, April encouraged Lara to begin the very essays that led to this book. April contributed her coaching talents to the creation of the chapter, Your Hopeful Life, by creating reflections for readers to search the meaning of their hopeful lives.

SARA OLSHER

PUBLISHING COORDINATOR

Sara Olsher is the founder and CEO of the family mental health and wellness company Mighty + Bright, and the author of nine picture books for kids coping with divorce, cancer, and change. As a single parent and cancer survivor, Sara's company provides tools and classes meant to help others navigate difficult times, with the goal of developing coping skills that will last a lifetime. Sara met Lara through a mutual friendship with April Stearns.

ALISON RASH

COVER ARTIST

Alison Rash is an artist and professor, who met Lara through April Stearns. Lara later hosted Alison on her podcast, My Hopeful Life. Alison relocated to Lincoln, Nebraska following her own MBC breast cancer diagnosis, after living and working in Los Angeles for two decades. Alison began the Ripple Project in 2020 to inspire, encourage and notice the ripples that each of us cast, believing that together we can create waves and make an impact. She has exhibited her art in Los Angeles, New York, San Francisco, San Diego, Dallas, and Washington D.C., as well as internationally.

hope scarves

Hope Scarves is an international non-profit organization based in Louisville, Kentucky. Our mission is to support people facing cancer through scarves, stories, and research.

Since our founding in 2012, we've grown exponentially and have affectionately become known as "The Sisterhood of the Traveling Scarves."

We collect scarves from around the world and stories from cancer survivors and pair them together to spread hope to others in treatment. They are the tangible reminders there is light in the world. They are our "now."

In addition to scarves and stories, Hope Scarves has established a Metastatic Breast Cancer Research Fund to support cutting edge researchers and clinical trials around the country. The research is the push for change, and it is our "future." Research is key for improved treatment options and outcomes.

To donate or learn more about the Hope Scarves mission, please visit

HOPESCARVES.ORG

Made in the USA
Columbia, SC
25 January 2023

10393324R00100